ISMAᶜĪL R. AL FĀRŪQĪ
SELECTED ESSAYS

Ismaʿīl R. al Fārūqī
Selected Essays

IIIT
LONDON • WASHINGTON

IIIT
P.O. BOX 669, HERNDON, VA 20172, USA • www.iiit.org

LONDON OFFICE
P.O. BOX 126, RICHMOND, SURREY TW9 2UD, UK • www.iiituk.com

ISBN 978-1-56564-598-1

Layout and Design by Saddiq Ali
Printed in Malta by Gutenberg Press Ltd

CONTENTS

FOREWORD

SINCE HIS DEATH in 1986, the legacy of Professor Ismaʿīl Rājī al Fārūqī's thought and action continue to inform and impress discourse throughout the world. An authority on Islam and comparative religion these select essays published in honor of that legacy and intellectual output portray him as an extremely gifted scholar, able to fortify with formidable logic and rational scientific argument his thinking on a number of important and complex, subjects, challenging and evaluating with a broad sweep of the brush prevailing ideas and concepts, whilst maintaining a clear *tawḥīdī* perspective throughout.

Al Fārūqī recognized that the crisis of the modern world was the crisis of knowledge, and this crisis, he thought, could only be cured via a new synthesis of knowledge in an Islamic epistemological framework, in order to galvanize Muslims to become active participants in intellectual life and contribute to it from an Islamic perspective. He worked tirelessly towards this end until his untimely demise.

The subjects discussed are not easy to grasp and the language Al Fārūqī employs is highly specialized, but it is hoped that for the most part both general and specialist readers alike will benefit from the perspectives offered and the overall issues examined. Each paper has been published as it first appeared with the caveat that diacritical marks have been added in accordance with our *Style Sheet*.

Since its establishment in 1981, the IIIT has served as a major center to facilitate serious scholarly efforts. Towards this end it has, over the decades, conducted numerous programs of research, seminars and conferences as well as publishing scholarly works specializing in the social sciences and areas of theology which to date number more than seven hundred titles in English and Arabic, many of which have been translated into other major languages.

JANUARY, 2018

BRIEF BIOGRAPHY OF
Ismaʿīl Rājī al Fārūqī
(1921–1986)

ISMAʿĪL RĀJĪ AL FĀRŪQĪ was born in Jaffa, Palestine. He was a great contemporary scholar of Islam and his scholarship encompassed the whole spectrum of Islamic Studies covering areas such as the study of religion, Islamic thought, approaches to knowledge, history, culture, education, interfaith dialogue, aesthetics, ethics, politics, economics, science and women's issues. It is no exaggeration to say that his was indeed a remarkably encyclopedic mind, and that he himself was a rare personality among contemporary Muslim scholars.

Al Fārūqī at first emigrated to Beirut, Lebanon, where he studied at the American University of Beirut, enrolling the following year at Indiana University's Graduate School of Arts and Sciences, to obtain an M.A. in philosophy in 1949. He was then accepted for entry into Harvard University's department of philosophy where he was awarded a second M.A. in philosophy in March 1951. However, he decided to return to Indiana University where he submitted his Ph.D. thesis to the department of philosophy obtaining his doctorate in September 1952. The title of his thesis was, "Justifying the Good: Metaphysics and Epistemology of Value."

Al Fārūqī then studied Islam in Cairo and other centers of Muslim learning, and Christianity at the Faculty of Divinity, McGill University. He taught at the Institute of Islamic Studies, McGill University; the Central Institute of Islamic Research, Karachi; the Institute of Higher Arabic Studies of the League of Arab States, Cairo University;

Al-Azhar University, Cairo; and at Syracuse University, USA, where he held the position of Associate Professor of Religion between 1964 and 1968, developing a program of Islamic Studies.

In the Fall of 1968 Al Fārūqī became professor of Islamic studies and history of religions in the Department of Religion, Temple University, a position he held until his tragic death in 1986.

The Problem of the Metaphysical Status of Values in the Western and Islamic Traditions

IN THE LAST hundred years, the problem of the metaphysical status of value has made great strides in the Western tradition. While insisting on the a priori nature of the moral law, Immanuel Kant sought to establish it as a "fact of reason."[1] The moral law is, according to him, both "a priori" and "given." From this position – a watershed in the history of Western philosophy – two traditions arose, one seeking to carry the Kantian insight deeper and further, and the other, seeking to establish a different insight because it denied Kantian epistemology altogether. The former arose and developed in the land of Kant, in Germany, whereas the latter did so in England having never outgrown the skepticism of David Hume. These are the idealist and the empiricist traditions respectively.

In the idealist camp, the paradox of the moral law being "a priori" and "a fact" was receiving more and more sophisticated but constructionist deductions until the breakthrough of Edmund Husserl.[2] Armed with the tools of the new discipline, *i.e.*, of phenomenology, Max Scheler succeeded in breaking down the Kantian law that the a priori is always formal and only the formal can be a priori. He succeeded in establishing a *materiale* a priori which is the content of an emotional intuition a priori,[3] thus freeing value-theory from the fruitless fixation of seeking the moral in ever more abstractionist constructions of the mind, under which the post-Kantian idealists had laboured.[4] The road was hence laid open for a rehabilitation of the moral law to its transcendental status, not as a demand of a confused Church Dogmatics which ambivalently held the finality of reason *and* its subservience to an ecclesiastical magisterium, but critically, as the content of an a priori *logique* of reason.[5] The foremost thinker who rose to the new challenge and promise of this great breakthrough in the Western idealist tradition and achieved this rehabilitation of value as an a priori, absolute, ideally self-existent essence endowed, like a genuine entelechy, with efficacious moving power and appeal, was Nikolai Hartmann.[6]

In his brilliant *Metaphysik der Erkenntniss*,[7] Nikolai Hartmann devoted a chapter in the last section of the last volume to the cognition of the valuational element in the external world. He rightly said that when a real-existent – be it a sensory object, an event or a situation, or an imagined picture, percept, or attitude – enters our consciousness, three levels of cognition are at once set into activity. First, there is the level on which we grasp the object presented to our consciousness. This is not a simple act, but a double-phased one. Besides apprehending by means of the senses the physical data of the object of cognition, there is the other phase in which we order by means of our noetical faculty the manifold data of sense under a frame constituting the form, essence or idea of the object apprehended. These two phases or modalities of cognition, the sensory and the noetic, constitute our theoretical cognition. Besides this level, cognition takes place on a second, totally different one; and it too is double-phased. Along with the theoretical apprehension of it, the object evokes in us attitudes of approval or disapproval, of acceptance or rejection, of desire, interest, quiescence, or of resistance and aversion. These are the data of valuational perception. As such they are "hard," as empirical as the sensory data; and the first phase consists in our apprehension of them, in our feeling these affections. In another phase or modality, the subject orders these data under the frame of an axiological idea or essence, of a *value*, which then becomes, in the subject's perception, the ground or "*pries*" of the object's valueness. As in the case of theoretical cognition there is no intuition of essences without the manifold data of sense, so in valuation cognition there is no intuition of value without the manifold data of interest, approval, desire, rejection, etc. For the act of approval, of desire, of being for or against itself implies a principle under which the attitude is taken. It is an entirely different matter whether such principle becomes in turn object of the theoretical consciousness on a third higher level, as when we reflect introspectively upon that which has determined our feeling or desiring or satisfaction when the object entered into our consciousness. This third stage may or may not be clear; indeed it may not be reached at all. For it is the prerogative of the moral teacher and investigator whose very business is to reflect on our value-apprehensions and to sift the various elements that determine and constitute them. But that the principle or essence under which our valuational act had taken place is there, and that it has determined the act or attitude in question – and that is all that is meant by the second stage of axiological cognition – remains indubitable. Theoretical (*i.e.*, discursive) consciousness of that under which the attitude is taken, is a tertiary affair. The primary object of axiological cognition is that which dominates the consciousness of the subject, namely, the real-existent object apprehended. The secondary object of axiological cognition is the value, the "*prius*" under which that which we perceive as good, is good. Such secondary cognition accompanies every primary cognition of goodness, every desiring and every averting. For no object of desire or aversion is ever apprehended except as falling under this or that value. If it were apprehended merely as affecting us as perceiving subjects in this or that manner, that is to say, as merely evoking in us this or that feeling-state, we would certainly be justified in describing our own feeling-states, but never the object as "cause" or "occasion" of these feeling-states. We may then speak of the stream or flux of affective states, but never of objects as good or bad. In this case, there would be little sense in talking of any real-existent, of any object as evoking the valuational act or attitude. To have good and bad objects, right and wrong acts and attitudes, implies therefore the entry into consciousness, though not into discursive consciousness, of something extra-personal, extra-feeling states, of something new which has determined the personal emotional response to be what it is.[8] It is such secondary cognition that Hartmann calls "the primary consciousness of value."[9] It consists neither in the feeling-states, nor in the discursive consciousness which relates feeling-states to valuational judgments;

but, rather, in the consciousness that value-objects are realizations, or instantiations, of certain values. Admittedly, it is a bit confusing to call it "primary consciousness of value." But we can appreciate that by calling it so, Hartmann meant to emphasize its immediacy, the fact that it provides the data which can become, by means of a later process of abstraction, the object of the theoretical consciousness, not on the level of sense, but on that level where consciousness is of that which has determined the emotional response once the sensory object has been subsumed thereunder. Secondly, the "primary consciousness of value" is *consciousness* because it is genuine knowledge of being. For its object is just as independent a reality as spatial relations are for geometrical knowledge, or bodies are for knowledge concerning things.[10] Values are objects of possible value-apprehension; but they do not come into being in the apprehension of them. Neither are they the attitudes of feeling-states of the perceiving subject, nor his thoughts and representations. On the contrary, it is they that determine the subject in his perception of them, while in themselves they remain utterly unaffected by whether or not they are perceived, perceived correctly or falsely, given real existence or violated. It is the fact that value-perception – though it is the emotional aspect of it that is there in question, not the sensory or the discursive – is an objective perception of genuine being that gives value-consciousness its gnoseological as well as ontological weight.[11]

This was a truly great achievement. Because of it, it has become possible in the idealist tradition, to speak critically of an aprioristic realm of being, namely the realm of values, whose members act as the first principles of all finalistic *nexūs* and command the deflection of given causal threads of nature, or the inception of new causal threads, realizing their real-existential *matériaux*. This realm of being, a priori though *materiale* or contentual, absolute though relational to man and all the realm of real existents, alive with real energizing power that takes the form of the moral ought, is a transcendent realm. Yet, it is not the cold, unreachable "other" that merely coexists with empirical reality,[12] but one that is of fundamental relevance to that reality. The fact that its relevance assumes the form of an ought or command tempts man to speak of it in personalist terms. Only a consistently critical attitude of the mind can keep present in consciousness the fact that the realm in question is really an infinite plenum of essences which, though tangentially moving and energizing, hover over reality at infinite distance. Their relevance is forever individual, pertaining to each value as an individual entelechy. As a realm, they are known only conceptually, by the discursive intuition of a fastidious reason.

In the empiricist camp, on the other hand, the a priori nature of the moral law was ruled out. Hence, its factual character was sought either in the psychic faculties of man or in the empirical qualities of things. In the former case, a wide variety of theories were elaborated; but they all based themselves in final analysis on goodness being a category under which real-existents are classified on account of man's being affected towards them in this or that fashion. The moral sentiment theories spoke of a sixth sense – the moral – which works spontaneously in man telling him what is good and what is evil.[13] The social approbative theories spoke of harmony or coherence with social convention as constitutive of goodness.[14] A third group which includes evolutionists, Marxists, pragmatists and humanists, spoke of reality as an interminable process and of the good as that which in any given stage of the process, agrees with the realities of that stage as well as with the onward moving logic which seeks to transcend the given stage and bring forth a new one.[15] However varied the detail, dependence upon a state of the subject remains in all these theories the essential characteristic of value throughout. That this state is an approbative state, or a state of agreement and harmony, demands in first place that the locus of goodness be within the subject alone. Indeed, it is a secondary question to determine the nature of that state of the subject, which is to be called 'good,' the first principle of these theories being that the good is a state of the subject at all. Taking this first principle for granted, another group of ethical theories – the psychological, properly speaking – defined the state of the subject that is constitutive of goodness as pleasure, affection or interest. Although all these theories derived some inspiration from Epicurus, only the first variety call themselves theories of hedonism; the second call themselves affective or emotive theories and the third, interest theories.[16] The psychological theories may be said to have gone deeper in their analysis than either the approbative or the process theories. For they have sought to analyze the rock-bottom element of which goodness supposedly consists. The analyses which these have made of the feelings of pleasure and pain, of the affective or emotive faculty, of interest and desire, are genuine contributions to psychology.

All these are empiricist theories because they conceive of value as a real-existent. A psychic state of the subject is a real-existent though psychic, since it is part of nature, of space-time, and is identifiable and explicable as an effect of certain antecedent natural causes, and a cause of certain consequent natural effects, in space-time. The empiricist nature of these theories has been acknowledged by all; and all but the French social approbative theories and the Marxist process theories which nonetheless agree with the basic premises of empiricism, have been recognized as standing squarely within the tradition of British Empiricism incepted by Locke, Berkeley and Hume. But nowhere has this empiricist nature of value been as clearly established and emphasized as in the writings of Clarence Irving Lewis. Indeed, compared with Lewis, many of the so-called empiricist theories do not seem empirical at all but verge, as in the case of the Marxist and the humanist theories, on the aprioristic.

In his *Analysis of Knowledge and Valuation*,[17] C. I. Lewis elaborated a naturalistic theory of valuation where, to use his own terms, "valuation represents one type of empirical cognition."[18] Like all empirical truth, the knowledge of value is empirical because it "cannot be known except, finally, through presentations of sense... (and rests), at bottom, on direct findings of sense."[19] However, unlike the presentations of outer sense, the presentations in question are given to the inner sense of desire, aversion and the feelings of pleasure and pain. In either case, the nature of value-knowledge is the same. According to Lewis, a naturalistic conception of values implies, therefore, "that valuations represent one type of empirical cognition, [and] hence [that] their correctness answers to a kind of objective fact, but one which can be learned only from experience and is not determinable a priori."[20] Equally, an empiricist axiology implies that "the quality by reference to which, ultimately, all things are to be judged valuable or disvaluable is a quality unmistakably identifiable in the direct apprehension of it when disclosed in experience."[21] Borrowing the expression of Berkeley, C. I. Lewis says that the *esse* of value is its *percipi*, for the only intrinsically valuable thing in existence is goodness discerned or discernable when disclosed in experience.[22] This apprehension, or rather consummation, of value-quality in experience is his hard datum. It is not adequately described as pleasure or pain, "hedonic tone," "quiescence pattern" or "satisfaction," because it is more general and includes them all. Although such expressions may help to characterize value, they never constitute it. For it is the state of the apprehending subject when value-quality is presented to his consciousness. This state is a kind of quiescence which the subject suffers when value enters his consciousness not as a meaning but as an experienced reality. That X is valuable, means, therefore, that upon its becoming an object of experience, its valuableness will be apprehended by the subject immediately. Such apprehension which is certainly "a mode of feeling" is "the head and front of the whole matter and no more precise test of objective value would be true to our intent."[23] Arguing against the apriorists, Lewis asserts that immediate value-apprehension in experience, such as might be the subject-matter of an expressive value-proposition (of the type, 'Now that I eat the ice cream, I apprehend directly a value-quality in the experience') is the basis of all valuation. "Without the experience of felt-value and disvalue, evaluations in general would have no-meaning."[24] Therefore, concludes Lewis, "the supposition that values are a priori could arise only through confusion between apprehension of a meaning itself and apprehension that this meaning has application in a particular instance... Only apprehensions of this latter sort are valuations."[25]

We must immediately notice that when Lewis's valuational 'hard datum' is expressed in propositions of the terminating type (*i.e.*, of the type, 'If S, then P' or 'If I eat icecream, I shall apprehend a value'), it has all the elements which constitute Hartmann's primary consciousness of value. Lewis's terminating proposition presupposes a feeling-state, an object that is necessarily related to the feeling-state, and a consciousness of that necessary relation – all of which are the elements of which

Hartmann's value-consciousness consists. Where Lewis differs from Hartmann is in the nature of the theoretical consciousness on second level, where the findings of the primary consciousness of value are translated into discursive propositions. Whereas Hartmann regards these propositions as a priori (*i.e.*, as expressing something that is originally given as content of an immediate intuition, when we disregard "every kind of positing of subjects which think them and of the actual conditions of such subjects, and also, when we disregard every kind of positing of objects to which they may apply," an experience of them being an experience of phenomenological whatness),[26] Lewis regards them as non-terminating propositions (*i.e.*, of the form SP = *Qn'* R*n*; or '*X* is good means that an indefinite number of propositions are true each of which says that if a certain act is performed, a certain value-quality will be apprehended in experience') that may find as much corroboration in experience, and therefore probability, as its Q's and R's find fulfilment when put to the test of experience.[27] But both Hartmann and Lewis are one in their anchoring of valuation in the given of experience, in a hard datum. Hartmann's epistemology enabled him to identify this given as *Wesen* or essence.[28] This was an answer to the question of the metaphysical status of value, which remains in Hartmann's mind the first question of value-theory. Had Lewis addressed himself to the same question, his empiricism would have caused him to seek an empirical value-quality in things. For it is inconsequential to claim that value is a state of the soul of the apprehending subject evoked by the presentation of an object in experience, without raising the question of the nature of that which, whether in the object or in the experience, causes the value-quality apprehension to be experienced. Here two answers are possible. Either our apprehension of value-quality in experience is an auto-suggested, auto-fabricated psychic illusion, or it is a quality or force in objects on a par with colour, size, gravity, magnetism, and other forces of nature. Only in these answers would a thorough-going empiricism be maintained. The first alternative will have to deny the whole of the real world and relegate it to a moment in "the stream of consciousness;" the other would have to explain how and why science has never been able to discover, isolate or study the so-called real value-force of an object in nature. By not addressing himself to this question at all, as far as this reader can make of his writings on the subject,[29] C. I. Lewis must have allowed his empirical value-quality of things to pass as a *qualilas occulla*.

Despite these splendid achievements on both fronts, that of idealism or apriorism as well as that of empiricism, the problem of the metaphysical status of value still stands removed from a lasting and satisfactory solution. In the idealist camp, values have remained floating essences which, though related to one another, sometimes closely and oft remotely, had no frame or structure that may be said to belong constitutively to their realm. We do not know them as a realm, despite the fact that we can have something to say about their status. For by definition, values are here regarded as transcendent beings forever removed from human knowledge. All that can be known of them is two modalities: the "ought-to-be," or the relevance of that value as such to the realm of real-existence, and the "ought-to-do," or the relevance of that value to a moral subject standing in the historic situation where the "ought-to-be" is relevant.[30] Indeed, we may never hope for a knowledge of the realm of values as such as intimate and penetrating as our knowledge of any individual member of the realm. Such knowledge of the whole as is claimed by the metaphysical personalists and theologian ethicists is, as Hartmann himself pointed out in criticism of his master Scheler, always a construct, and can never aspire to a critical establishment of its tenets.[31] As a realm, human knowledge of them will remain as unrewarding as George Santayana's bold and philosophically critical description of the "Realm of Essence."[32] Furthermore, as Hartmann himself has pointed out, the realm of values is one where individual members operate under the law of the *bellum omnium contra omnes*; for every individual member is constantly trying to monopolize the field of human vision and rule tyrannically to the exclusion of its brother-members without any chance of reconciliation whatever.[33] The idealist tradition, therefore, which claims ideal self-existence *sui generis* for values,[34] does so for them as an indefinite internally chaotic mass, despite the fact that many significant internal relationships are discernible and of which a "Phenomenology of values" is even possible.[35]

While Hartmann remained true to the phenomenological method and denied himself any step beyond the description of some value-relationships, Scheler could not resist the temptation to look for an inner structural principle in the realm of values, and he identified that principle as saintliness.[36] This turned out to be the one final value which determines the valueness of all other values. This, Scheler has done at the cost of destroying the phenomenologicality of the description; for the raising of saintliness to the rank of axiological supremacy led to the suspicion – which Scheler never answered – that saintliness was really the only value and all other "values" were categorical means to it. It was this finding which put him squarely within the Christian camp where theology was only too anxious and happy to back him up and to appropriate his discoveries.[37] On the other hand, Hartmann's critical strictness safeguarded the philosophical gains he had achieved against such speculation. But it left his value-realm, despite the excellent "phenomenology of value," devoid of inner unity. Every value is practically a God unto man; and there is no overarching value to bring them under control and harmony.[38]

On the other hand, assuming the object of consciousness, or the value itself, out of bounds for investigation and research, the empiricist camp directed its attention to the apprehending subject. The psychologists analyzed his apprehensions of value-quality, *i.e.*, his attitudes, desires and aversions, and the philosophers reduced their task to that of semantically analyzing what the subject means to say when he reports his findings of value-quality. The former have availed themselves of the findings of empirical psychology and elaborated on the basis of its data their hedonistic, affective and interest theories. The latter were predominantly the logical positivists who assumed that no proposition is meaningful unless it is analytic (and hence, tautological, claiming no more than that such predicate is conventionally used in a given language to mean what it asserts) or synthetic (and hence, empirical, claiming a greater or lesser degree of probability such as any testable generalization of science might possess).[39] From this, the logical positivists moved on to the assertion that the propositions of ethics belong to neither category, and are hence meaningless.[40] According to them, moral predicates are mere expressions of emotions, equivalent to the more familiar exclamations and interjections of 'Oh,' 'Hurrah' and 'Alas.'[41] Moral propositions are thus removed outside the realms of truth and falsehood, and there is no way in which a conscious, deliberate and consistently-held difference in what ought or ought not to be, can be solved or even composed.[42]

The foregoing may be said to be an account of the secular side of the Western Tradition of thought in the field of metaphysics of value. There is no doubt, however, that the said side is the greater, for it includes most of the thinking that has taken place in the West. That thinking which is specifically Christian has not produced much on this question. True to type, modern Christian thought in this as well as in other fields has come hobbling after secular thought in what may be described as an attempt by Christian scholars to react, adjust to, or appropriate the achievements of secular thought.

As far as is known to this author, only two Christian thinkers have made a deliberate attempt to "benefit" theology from the achievements of secular thought in the problem of the metaphysical status of values, namely, Edgar S. Brightman[43] and Henry N. Wieman.[44] The former borrowed heavily from Max Scheler and followed him into metaphysical personalism: the latter borrowed heavily from Ralph Barton Perry and constructed what came to be called an "empirical theology." At the same time that Wieman was trying to explore the possibilities of a wedding of empiricism to theology, Brightman was reacting against the introduction of this empiricism into the stream of American thought.

Against Perry, he argued for a rejection of the view that value is the object of an interest, on the grounds that it subjects the whole realm of value to dependence on consciousness. This is subjectivism, he maintained, as it makes a state of the subject constitutive of value.[45] Brightman saw that though all value may be relational to consciousness, it is not relative thereto.[46] But the establishment of the realm of value as an objective real realm beyond consciousness was indispensable for making sense of religious experience.[47] That realm, he held, is the very "principle by which the mind tests and seeks to organize its religious experience."[48] But this realm of objective value can be only "the conscious experience and will of one Supreme Person, God."[49] Drawing on Sorley[50] as well as on Scheler, Brightman defined "the objectivity of values… (as meaning) their existence as purposes of the Divine Mind."[51]

The first premise of Brightman's philosophy, his concern to prevent the realm of values from being subjective – that is to say, from an essential dependence on human consciousness – is worthy and well taken. But the second premise of his philosophy, his identification of values with the ideas and purposes of a Supreme Person, lacks the wisdom of his negative first premise. Just as the relationality of values to human consciousness does not make them the product of that consciousness, their relationality to a Supreme Mind – if such can be established – does not make them that Mind's factitive "ideas and purposes." At best, they would be relational to it; and it would be as objectively determined by them as human consciousness. Once they are taken to be the factitive product of any consciousness, whether human or divine, their objective reality is in real danger. Secondly, the personalization of the Godhead stands on a par with that of the cosmos. The phenomenon of the human person willing, desiring, judging and acting in freedom and responsibility is a fact. It is the only fact of its kind. Reading this fact into the cosmos, the Godhead or any other non-man is unwarranted construction, a leap outside the realm of critical thought.

Viewed from another angle, Brightman's inconsequence consisted in saving the objectivity of value by loosening the grip of consciousness upon it, and tossing that realm, as it were, onto the upper stage of divine consciousness. Wieman, on the other hand, sought to save that same objectivity by subjecting the realm of value to the specific structures constituting the experience of nature by that human consciousness. The one tried to save objectivity by raising and expanding, the other by lowering and reducing.

Wieman was sufficiently interested in R. B. Perry to write his doctoral dissertation on Perry's theory of value as interest. His acceptance of Perry's metaphysic of value was complete.[52] He added to it, however, the Bergsonian notion of creativity, and attributed this notion not to any interest, however general and inclusive – as Perry did – but, to the principle of organization of all interests, which is not itself an interest unless the term is stretched beyond its common sense meaning. A third and special affinity to Josiah Royce becomes evident when we consider that, for Wieman, what is involved in the organization of interests is not a principle but an event, a "creative event." The plea for objectivity begins with the identification of interest with "the total process of interaction between organism and environment,"[53] and hence, with the implication that it does not wholly depend upon the subject, and is therefore not entirely a state of the subject. An attempt to confirm this objectivity followed with an analysis of the possibility of achieving the "creative event" of interest-organization on the social level. Such a solution was precisely Perry's.[54] But this had to be abandoned as unworkable when Wieman examined the concrete example of Western society and found reason not only "to doubt the reality of a free society (in which mutual creativity can be fully operative, but) even its possibility."[55] This failure of society to measure up to the requirements led Wieman to "look beyond society for that organization of interests which will yield the largest measure of good" and this, he asserted, is religion.[56] For, religion encompasses all interests and pursues them as "cosmic purpose;"[57] God as "individuality and teleology of the universe;" etc.[58] However, in order to accommodate the Christian dogma of redemption in this secularization of religion and empirical "cosmic purpose" (*sic*) Wieman now turned against the individuality and personal character of interest to assert that cosmic interest may never be a proper object of any man's interest and pursuit, for it stands beyond human control and must transcend the human range of experience and interest. Consequently, man's ultimate role can be only one of total acquiescence in the divine scheme.[59]

It is nothing short of amazing to the rational observer how this superlatively empiricist mind can go on asserting the empiricist thesis while at the same time denying it in favour of articles of dogmatic faith. As late as the appearance of *The Empirical Theology of Henry Nelson Wieman*, Wieman wrote that outside what is given to sense, nothing divine, religious or moral could be sought or found.[60] This notwithstanding, he spoke of another knowledge, immediate and subjective, whose object constitutes a realm a *part*, different from and in every respect other than the realm which empirical science studies. He even gave them the contrasting names of form and content asserting that, while the former was best developed by the modern West, and the latter by the ancient East, truth is really in a merging of the two.[61] But the only reason he gave for the existence and validity of the new source of knowledge is the old argument that there must be a mind and a person in order to have any scientific knowledge at all.[62] It is no wonder that he made this concession under the criticism of his colleague, Professor Bernard Eugene Meland. Aiming at Wieman's notion of the never-to-be-experienced cosmic purpose which is God asserted alongside the empiricist thesis, the latter wrote with a charity that is all the more devastating because it is charitable: "what he (Wieman) once spoke of as the 'rich fullness of experience' presents a constant 'more' to him, which is the unmanageable depth of the living situation, extending to the unmanageable dimensions (or inexperienceable aspect) of God's reality. To him, this is at once an *abundance of good* and a *threat to clarified understanding* of that which is ultimately good and transforming of our own good." Professor Meland rightly concluded that this is the work of a "divided mind," endowed with "dual loyalties."[63]

Thus the problem stands in the Western tradition.

Passing over to the Islamic tradition, we find that axiological phenomenology was pursued not as a philosophic discipline as such, but as one or another of the sciences of the Qur'an.[64] Axiological methodology, on the other hand, was pursued as the science of the *ṣifāt* (divine attributes). In the former, many of the so-called "*ᶜUlūm al Qur'ān*" were really searches after the underlying meanings of revelation and hence after that which God had intended to enter man's consciousness and determine his will; *i.e.*, after values, their inter-relations and structure. The preoccupation of the theorists of *asbāb al-nuzūl* with history, for instance, was a means for evaluating the contexts in which the verses were revealed; and this in turn led to a grasping of the divine meaning, or value, which God intended to convey.[65] In the latter, the question of the sense in which God's attributes are predicable of Him amounts really to that of the metaphysical status of value. For the *ṣifāt* were all the ethical ideals of the Muslim – to be sure, never completely realizable by man on earth or in heaven – but nonetheless constituting the ultimate ideals of truth, goodness and beauty.[66] In fact this predication of values or ideals to God as attributes saved the unity and objectivity of the Muslim's ideals in the sea of interpretations to which the word of God was subjected by authority-condemning Muslims. In the course of the spread of Islam east of the Two Rivers where Arabization did not keep abreast with Islamization, the Qur'anic meanings came to be less and less the object of an intuitive grasp and immediate understanding, and more and more that of a conceptualizing sense-empiricism in doubt about the new message which shattered its old pre-Islamic world-view. Compared with the Arab or fully-Arabicized mind, this mind was incapable of fully grasping the idea of transcendence and of appreciating the necessarily-human, necessarily-conceptual and necessarily-aesthetic (poetic) language in which the transcendent may be expressed or talked about. But where the transcendent or the Qur'anic meanings pertaining thereto are not object of an immediate intuition, they become irrational stumbling-blocks. It was natural therefore that among those whose consciousness has not been completely governed by the categories of Arab consciousness, a movement began to spread which understood God in anthropomorphic terms and which drew its intellectual nourishment either from Eastern Christianity, from the religions of Persia and India, or from the Jahwism of those Jews who thought of their God in excessively human terms.[67] Judging from the kind of arguments which the *Mushabbihah* (anthropomorphists) advanced in support of their position, we may even say that the converts from Judaism must have supplied the intellectual leadership of the other anthropomorphists who, according to Shahrastānī, consisted largely of *al-Shīʿah al-Ghāliyah*, or *Shīʿah* excessivists (*e.g.*, Ḥashwiyyah, Hishāmiyyah, Muḍar, Kuhmus, Aḥmad al-Hujaymī, etc.)[68] The *Mushabbihah* argued that "their God has a figure, organs and parts, some spiritual and some bodily; that He moves about, descends and ascends, sits down and stays put..." that "God's eyes once ailed Him and the angels cured their ailment, that He actually cried when the Deluge destroyed mankind until His eyes hurt Him: that the throne squeaks when He sits on it as a new saddle does when the rider sits on it," that "Moses... actually heard the voice of God and that it was thundering like the sound of dragging chains," etc.[69] "Pure anthropomorphism," he wrote, "is a purely Jewish affair, though not all Jews are anthropomorphists. It was mostly the Karaites among them that capitalized on the Torah's many words about God which [ostensibly] support their thesis."[70]

Against these, the adherents of the idea of transcendence rose like one man, but with several voices. Several schools were formed, each of which advanced arguments to prove its own view of things. However, all of them opposed the new anti-transcendentalist anthropomorphism with equal absoluteness and determination.

The stakes were high: If God were to be understood anthropomorphically, His attributes would be on a par with the attributes of men. They would certainly be the ideal and most perfect – as the attributes of the Greek deities – but their unity, objectivity and transcendent status would become meaningless as they are taken to be the unparalleled but not unparallelable, admirable but not necessary, perfections of man. The new position pulls down the two houses at once: that of theology and that of ethics; of *tawḥīd*, or the unitarianism of God, and of the transcendent status of the ethically imperative or the ethical (*i.e.*, non-empirical) nature of the command.

Maʿbad al-Juhanī and Ghaylān ibn Marwān were the first to pose the problem as one of divine attributes.[71] Seized with spiritual panic when they saw the new converts entertain their anthropomorphic conception of the Godhead, Maʿbad and Ghaylān argued for transcendence by denying all the divine attributes. Although this opinion later developed into a school of philosophy, their argument was simple enough. God, they are reputed to have said, along with the Muʿtazilah school, "is knowing in His essence, capable in His essence, alive in His essence, not by means of [a faculty] of knowledge, [a faculty] of capacity, [a faculty] of life. These attributes are eternal in Him; they are meanings belonging to Him. For, if they co-existed with Him [as faculties] in eternity – which is the central core of the Godhead – they would have shared with Him the divine status."[72] The Divine attributes are thus *muʿaṭṭalah* or neutralized. "It is impossible that there be two uncreated, eternal beings," and it is certain, according to them, that "whoever established a meaning or an attribute as eternal, has actually established the existence of two gods."[73] On these lines, the *Muʿaṭṭilah*, or those who neutralize the divine attributes, argued that the attributes are not predicative of God, but definitive; that to predicate them of God is only a means of talking about Him.

A more sophisticated version of the argument was advanced by Abū al-Hudhayl al-ʿAllāf. "He" (*i.e.*, God), he said, "is knowing with a knowledge which is Himself, capable with a capacity which is Himself, alive with a life which is Himself; and so is the case with divine hearing, seeing, eternity, glory, might, greatness, magnanimity and all the other attributes of His self... When I say 'God is knowing,' I simply assert that He has knowledge which is God and have denied that He has ignorance [which is not God]; I have pointed to a known that has been or is existent (*wa-dalaltu ʿalā maʿlūm kāna aw yakūnu*). And when I say 'God is capable,' I have simply denied God's incapacity, asserted that He has a capacity which is God himself and pointed to a something that is the object of that capacity."[74] All this boils down to a repudiation of the literal meaning of the Qur'anic attribution for a figurative one. Indeed, al-Ashʿarī tells us that "Abū al-Hudhayl said so himself. 'God has a face,' he said, 'which is Himself; it is He, and so is His soul.' He interprets allegorically the Qur'anic assertion regarding the divine hand as meaning a blessing, and '...in order that you might be formed under Mine eye' (Qur'an, 20:39) as meaning 'with My knowledge.'"[75] Transcendence was thus preserved, but at the cost of *taʿṭīl* or neutralization.

This procedure was as much followed by the Qadariyyah, or those who hold man capable of action and hence ethically responsible, as the Jabriyyah or determinists. The former were also known as Muʿtazilah for holding a number of other views. They were compelled to "neutralize" because of the consideration that if God's acting was literally true of Him, He would have to be, in some respect, the efficient cause of becoming in nature. Such involvement of God in nature, *i.e.*, His being the author of change, would not only compromise His immutability or ontological poise, but the ethical responsibility of man. For man's actions too are events in nature; and as long as this realm is not exclusively that of man alone, human responsibility would be impaired. Anxious to save this ethical responsibility, the Qadariyyah had at least to restrict the meaning of divine action. On the other hand, the Jabriyyah were compelled to neutralize the divine attributes because, they argued, to hold them true of God is to project unto Him schemata of character which are empirically given in man and which have thence been borrowed to build our concept of Him. This is tantamount to anthropormorphizing Him. "We should not," said Jahm ibn Ṣafwān, "describe God by that which is true of His creatures."[76] Thus, the Jabriyyah lay the grounds for neutralization. God is not "alive" or "knowing," because these are human attributes. And yet, God is certainly capable and acting because these are not at all prerogatives of man – man being a God-determined creature throughout.[77] Evidently, they were anxious to deny God all the attributes which smack of human character or colour; and for this reason, they first divided them into definitive and predicative attributes of divine Being. The former they called *ṣifāt al-dhāt*, or "attributes of the divine Self," the latter, *ṣifāt al-fiᶜl*, or "attributes of divine action."[78] Their object was to save transcendence from the charge that if action and knowledge were predicative, change in the divine Being as subject of action, which is a necessary implication of the processes of knowing and acting, would be inevitable.[79] Hence, they readily agreed with their opponents to effect the same *taᶜṭīl*, or neutralization, upon all predicative attributes by allegorically interpreting them. When they turned to the definitive attributes, allegorical interpretation was not so successful, since the content was already an abstract one. Hence, they had recourse to the alternative of identifying the definitive attributes with the divine Self. Whereas the Qadariyyah neutralized in order to save human freedom and responsibility, the Jabriyyah did so in order to deny that freedom and responsibility.

With all the divine attributes thus *muᶜaṭṭalah*, or explained away by neutralization, they thought the attributes would pose no problem at all and divine transcendence would be maintained.

However, this process of *taᶜṭīl*, to which all the arguments of the Jabriyyah and Qadariyyah really boil down, ran counter to the intuitive grasp of Qur'anic meaning by those whose consciousness has remained true to the categories of the Arabic Qur'an. For these, it was no problem to accept the verbatim character of revelation, without anthropomorphism. No wonder then that, while the anthropomorphism of the *Mushabbihah* (anthropomorphists) revolted them, the rationalizations and strained allegorical interpretations of the *Muʿaṭṭilah* (neutralizationists) left them not only unmoved but troubled. What they looked for was an intellectually satisfying view that would establish at once the transcendent character of deity as well as the *verbatim* meaning of the attributes as stated in the Qur'an.[80] Mālik ibn Anas, Sufyān al-Thawrī, Aḥmad ibn Ḥanbal and Dāwūd ibn ʿAlī al-Iṣfahānī are said to have held this view.[81] But it was ʿAbdullāh ibn Saʿīd al-Kullābī that first put this point of view discursively.[82] God's attributes are necessary, he reasoned, because He ascribed them to Himself in the Qur'an which is His work. God, he thought, does indeed have a hand, for example; but it is far from being a human hand. Likewise, God is knowing and has knowledge, but the how of His knowing must forever escape us.[83]

It was this candid and yet unsophisticated intuition of the *ṣifātiyyah* (or attributists; *i.e.*, upholders of the real though not anthropomorphic truth of the attributes) that Abū al-Ḥasan al-Ashʿarī seized upon, elaborated and gave to posterity as definitive of the Islamic position.[84] The attributes, he claimed, imply no change in the deity and are co-eternal with the divine Being. Hence they are Him. But they are certainly not Him inasmuch as He stands beyond all human knowledge and hence, beyond all assertions about the divine. As his famous dictum went, "the divine attributes are eternal, inhering in the divine Self. Neither can it be said that they [the attributes] are Him; nor that they are other than Him; neither that He is not them, nor that He is other than them."[85] Historically, this brought about crushing silence to both *Mushabbihah* and *Muʿaṭṭilah*. None could contradict either horn of the argument, despite the fact that the argument as a whole still left most intellectuals unsatisfied with its simple and clear assertion and denial at the same time. And yet, anyone who dared object to it faced the impossible task of denying either God's transcendence or the *verbatim* revealed status of the Qur'an. However, couched in these very terms, the problem was bogged down forever. For by juxtaposing in antinomical alternation, the transcendence of the divine Essence, and the Qur'an's fact of predication of attributes to that essence, any solution was ruled out *ex hypothesi*. The direct and unequivocal attribution of the *ṣifāt* to God is true because it is Qur'anic. And yet, as long as the *ṣifāt* are taken as if to instruct us about God *in esse*, *i.e.*, from an ontological point of view, they run diametrically opposed to the transcendental character of the Godhead, which is an equally Qur'anic position, and which emphasizes that "...there is nothing like unto Him,..." (Qur'an, 42:11).

Obviously, the fault lay in couching the problem as one of whether or not the attributes instruct us about God's essence, about His ontological being. Al-Ashʿarī's antinomy of the attributes being and not-being God, does not solve the problem. It merely asserts the two truths that the attributes, being Qur'anic, must be true of God; and that being conceptual, *i.e.*, belonging to human knowledge, they cannot *ex hypothesi* instruct about God's transcendent being. The antinomic relation remains bogged down, and so does the problem of the attributes.

Although Ashʿarism had its great men, it had greater opponents. Indeed, it has been elbowed out as an aberration verging on heresy and has never seen a bright day since al-Ghazālī gave it a crushing refutation in favour of Sufism.[86] Despite this fact, the fundamental al-Ashʿarī position regarding the divine attributes remained constitutive of all orthodox Islamic positions throughout, including that of Sufism. Indeed, al-Ghazālī's argument regarding the *ṣifāt* did not go at all beyond the denial of anthropomorphism (hence the refutation of the *mushabbihah* in favour of the *ṣifātiyyah*) and the assertion of the literal truth of the attributes (and hence, the refutation of the Muʿtazilī and other neutralizationists' identification of the attributes with divine Essence).[87] This is all Ashʿarist doctrine to the core; and the overthrow of Ashʿarism by Sufism has not added anything new to the argument. As long as the question remained one of ontology, that is of the being, as such, of God, no solution was ever possible. As the great Kant had found out, the being of the transcendent is a realm forever removed from human knowledge and conceptualization.[88] Hence, the Qur'anic predication of the attributes to the being of God is, though absolutely true, a philosophic stumbling block which is not removed by merely asserting it.

Theology can escape it only at the cost of criticality.

And yet, it is certainly within the tradition of *kalām* that the direction of a solution to the antinomy must be sought. For what went wrong with the Islamic answer to the problem of the *ṣifāt* is the form in which the Muslim theologians have presented the problem. Al-Ashʿarī was, in a way, compelled to pose the problem as he did in order to save transcendence. And once the problem was posed in the form al-Ashʿarī gave to it, nobody in the Islamic tradition could carry it forward towards a solution. What was needed is, above all, a change of perspective.

Of all the Islamic thinkers who addressed themselves to the problem of the *ṣifāt*, none had the breadth to shake the problem from its Ashʿarite fixation except Taqiyy al-Dīn Aḥmad ibn Taymiyyah. It was he who opened the road to a solution of al-Ashʿarī's antinomy. Not that he had actually solved it but that he lifted it from the fixation under which it lay immobile for centuries. It is sufficient for Ibn Taymiyyah's immortal credit that he has done precisely no more than to remove the problem out of the ontological fixation in which al-Ghazālī had left it.

Firstly, Ibn Taymiyyah seconded the Orthodoxy's rejection of the *Muʿaṭṭilah*, on the grounds of the predication of attributes to God by the Qur'an whose attributism is sufficiently evident. This is a good *ṣifātī* position. The nature of God could not be better known by anyone than by God Himself. Even the Prophet's personal knowledge of God could not compare with divine knowledge. This knowledge is given to us in the Qur'an; for it was He who has therein described His nature. His word about Himself is therefore the first and last word.[89]

Secondly, the Jabriyyah have emphasized a very true principle, namely, that we may not predicate of God anything that is predicable of man. That is the principle of transcendence which remains the head and fount of all Islam as well as the doctrinal mainstay of "the people of the *Sunnah*, of *Jamāʿah* and of *Ḥadīth*, the companions of Mālik, Shāfiʿī, Abū Ḥanīfah, Aḥmad [ibn Ḥanbal]... the predecessors of the *ummah*... that 'Nothing is like unto Him.'"[90] *Tanzīh*, or the transcendentalist conception of God, must be maintained.

Thirdly, Ibn Taymiyyah exposed the fact that both al-Ashʿarī's as well as his opponents' objection to and denial of the process of *taʿṭīl* was the direct effect of their fear to introduce plurality into the conception of God. But a unity of God which is absolutely opposed to plurality must be a mathematical unity; and it was precisely such arithmetic conception of unity that stood at the root of their denial of multiplicity or becoming in the Godhead, implied, according to them, in any acceptance of the attributes as real and belonging to divine essence. Divine unity, Ibn Taymiyyah thought, was organic, not mathematical; hence, there is no need to distinguish between predicative attributes pertaining to divine action and definitive attributes pertaining to essence or to identify the predicative attributes with that essence. "Divine essence is one," Ibn Taymiyyah argues, "and the attributes are many."[91] Indeed, the attributes are infinite in number, neither nine as the Ashʿarīs have thought, nor any other number.[92] "Mankind is incapable of ever bringing the divine attributes within definitive survey."[93] Nonetheless, their plurality does not affect the unity of divine essence. For it is nonsense to speak of many attributes without a unique being of whom they are the attributes. "That of whom a predicate is predicated cannot be the predicate;"[94] that is to say, in the same respect. If, Ibn Taymiyyah reasoned, we can and do conceive of a substance that is one but endowed with many attributes, and are incapable of conceiving of one that is endowed with none, it should be equally possible for us to conceive of a One God endowed with a manifold will that is not ontologically alternative to Him, but is in a sense other than the ontological "Him."[95]

Fourthly, while thus the process of thought which leads to neutralization is repudiated, Ibn Taymiyyah is equally anxious to refute the Ashʿarī consequences drawn from that process. Against al-Ashʿarī's "neither He nor other than He" Ibn Taymiyyah argued that "To speak of His attributes is a kind of [or tantamount to] speaking of His essence,"[96] thus establishing for the first time in the history of Islamic theology a differentiation within the concept of God, of two orders, to wit: The order of being and the order of knowing. Rejecting, therefore, the *Ṣifātiyyah's* attempt to safeguard transcendence by emptying the attributes of their content (*i.e.*, the fallacy of the deconcretissation of the concrete,[97] the concrete being in this case God) as idle, Ibn Taymiyyah accepted their multiplicity declaring it a multiplicity in knowledge which, as such, does not involve *shirk* (association of other eternal beings with God) because it does not pertain to God as He is in Himself, but as we know Him.

Fifthly, the divine attributes do not constitute an irrational order, but a rational and orderly one. We discern therein a hierarchical stratification, an order to rank; for the attributes are *tafāḍulī*.[98] This aspect of the attributes is, further, inseparable from their pluralism; for it is inconceivable that a pluralistic realm belonging to Divine essence should not be orderly and hence, hierarchical. Not that the attributes now belong to essence, not to act, as the Ashʿarīs and Muʿtazilah would have it, but that they all belong to the One Being in the same respect. The attributes stand in such relations to one another as to make them prior to others.

These insights of Ibn Taymiyyah constitute the greatest contribution to the problem of the *ṣifāt* to date. Together, their philosophical purport amounts to a change of the metaphysical status of the attributes. The attributes are all God's, to be sure; and they all are attributes of His essence, for to talk of them is to talk of God's essence inasmuch as that essence can become object of human knowledge. God *in esse*, we may therefore understand Ibn Taymiyyah as wanting to say, we may and shall never know. Being the transcendent Being, He can never become object of human knowledge. But He remains the only One Necessary Being prior to all other beings which are contingent and whose contingent reality is itself the proof of His being. God *in percipi*, on the other hand, may be the object of knowledge, and this is none other than the attributes which are partly given to us as the demands of reason, or implications of our empirical knowledge of the world and men. These are given to us in the Qur'anic revelation or in the *Ḥadīth*, as *akhbār*, which it is the duty of Muslims not only to accept in their common sense (*ẓāhir*) meaning while keeping in mind that they are modes of talking about Him intelligible to man, but to elaborate and analyze them seeking out their implications by concordance (*muṭābaqah*), material implication (*laḍāmun*) and formal implication (*iltizām*).[99] In either case, then, the attributes are "ideas of reason," informative about God inasmuch as He can be object of human knowledge at all. The old questions of the *Mutakallimīn*, Ibn Taymiyyah is here saying, were misconceived: All attributes have the same status, namely, they are God, not *in esse* since this remains the *mawṣūf* (He of whom the predicate is predicated) and no *mawṣūf* can be its own *ṣifāt*, but *in percipi*. They are infinite and, inasmuch as we can discern them, hierarchical.

To these insights we must add those gained from Ibn Taymiyyah's critique of sufism.[100] The sum of these which concern us here is that contrary to the *ittiḥādī* (unionist) claims, man can never unite with God in any fashion. All man can achieve in this world is obedience to divine command and compliance with divine will. For God, especially God *in esse*, we may never know, not to speak of uniting with Him. But His will is not only knowable – through God's own *ikhbār* (revelation) and reason's elaboration and analysis of the given in creation – but stands as a command which man ought to heed and realize. These are the same methods by which we know the *ṣifāt*. Furthermore, the *ṣifāt* are the ideals – ad *perfectum* – which human conduct ought to, but will never realize. As "ideas of reason," they serve to regulate human conduct by orienting it towards themselves. Contentually as well as methodologically, therefore, the *ṣifāt* are the divine will, and divine will is not God-in *esse*, but *God-in-percipi*, for all that is given to us to know of Him is His will, or *ṣifāt*. The *ṣifāt* or divine will are God-for-us, on the level of human knowledge while remaining mere attributes of a *mawṣūf* on the level of being.

Together, these insights point to the direction in which a solution of the problem of the metaphysical status of values may be sought. If the *ṣifāt* are values – and this can hardly be contested since the *ṣifāt* have constituted the regulative ideals of practical reason in the Islamic tradition – the Islamic tradition may be said to have accomplished through Ibn Taymiyyah's revolution what the Western idealist tradition has achieved through the phenomenological. Values – and likewise the *ṣifāt* – are ideally self-existent essences, whence the ought-to-be, or the ethically-imperative, issues. They are a pluralistic yet orderly and hierarchical realm of which a "phenomenology of values" is possible by the processes of *muṭābaqah*, *taḍāmun* and *iltizām*. The ought-to-be of values is all that can be known of them; they are, *in percipi*, this very ought. And so are the *ṣifāt*; for they become known to us in so far as God Himself becomes object of knowledge, but never *in esse*. The problem at which the wisdom of Nikolai Hartmann stopped, namely, the chaos inherent in the realm of values to which their individual tyranny and mutual antinomic relations give evidence, may at least be restated, and perhaps solved under the Islamic consideration that they are the will of a unique divine being – the transcendent whole of which they are, according to Hartmann, the members. The commands of a Being are one though many; and their inner conflicts may dissolve in the unity of the divine Being of Whom they are the will. But such unity of divine Being cannot be the unity of a Person – the mistake of metaphysical personalism. It is endowed with will; and that is the ought-to-be of value emitted by the ideal, a priori, transcendent realm. But this is not the will of a person. It is, rather, the 'moving appeal' of the realm and of its individual members, a modality of their ideal existence. The establishment of this insight for a philosophy that is committed to reason and criticality as well as to the *khabar* of the divine word, is the task par excellence of the theology of the future.

Notes

1. "The consciousness of this fundamental principle (the categorical imperative) may be called a fact of reason, since one cannot ferret it out from antecedent data of reason, such as the consciousness of freedom (for this is not antecedently given), and since it forces itself upon us as a synthetic proposition a priori based on no pure or empirical intuition." Kant, Immanuel, *Critique of Practical Reason*, V, 31, Lewis White Beck's translation, University of Chicago Press, Chicago, 1950, p. 142.
2. For a description of the currents of philosophical thinking leading to Husserl and Husserl's "breakthrough to phenomenology," see Farber, Marvin, *The Foundation of Phenomenology: Edmund Husserl and the Quest for a Rigorous Science of Philosophy*, Harvard University Press, Cambridge, 1943, pp. 3-222.
3. Scheler, Max, *Der Formalismus in der Ethik und die materiale Wertethik*, Jahrbuch fur philosophie und phänomenologische Forschung, Niemeyer, Halle, 1913-1916, Chap. IV, pp. 48 ff.
4. *E.g.*, Schelling, Fichte, Hegel, Schopenhauer.
5. Scheler, Max, *op. cit.*, pp. 85-87. It should be noted here that Hemsterhuis had by this time developed the concept of an *organe moral*, for the same purpose.
6. Hartmann, Nicolai, *Ethik*, 1926, translated by S. Colt under the title *Ethics*, George Allen und Unwin Ltd., London, 1932, Vol. I, pp. 183-247.
7. *Les principes d'une métaphysique de la connaissance*, Tome II, Aubier, Paris, 1946, pp. 282 ff.
8. Hartmann, *Ethics*, Vol. I, pp. 222-223.
9. Ibid., pp. 99-102.
10. Ibid., p. 219.
11. Ibid., p.226. Hartmann, *Les principes d'une metaphysique de la connaissance*, Tome I, pp. 281-284.
12. Such as "the Absolute Other" of Indian religions, or the impersonal god of some philosophers (e.g., Ibn Rushd).

13. Such are, for example, the theories of Edward Westermarck (*Ethical Relativity*, Harcourt, Brace and Co., Inc., New York, 1932; and *Christianity and Morals*, The MacMillan Co., New York, 1939), of Arthur Kenyon Rogers (*The Theory of Ethics*, The MacMillan Co., New York, 1934), of Frank Chapman Sharp (*Ethics*, The Century Co., New York, 1928), etc.
14. Such are, for example, the theories of Emile Durkheim (*On the Division of Labor in Society*, tr. by G. Simpson, The MacMillan Co., New York, 1933; and *The Elementary Forms of the Religious Life*, tr. by J. W. Swain, George Allen and Unwin, Ltd., London, 1915), and of Lucien Levy-Bruhl (*Ethics and Moral Science*, tr. by Elizabeth Lee, Archebald Constable and Co., Ltd. London, 1905), etc.
15. Examples of the first kind, *i.e.*, evolutionist, are Thomas H. Huxley (*Evolution and Ethics*, D. Appleton and Co., New York, 1929), Olaf Stapledon (*A Modern Theory of Ethics*, Methuen and Co., London, 1929), Peter Kropotkin (*Ethics, Origin and Development*, tr. by L. S. Friedland and J. R. Peroshnikoff, The Dial Press, New York, 1926), and Julian S. Huxley (*Evolutionary Ethics*, Oxford University Press, London, 1943). Of the second type, *viz.*, Marxist, are Karl Marx and Friedrich Engel's writings. Of the third type, *i.e.*, pragmatist, are John Dewey (*Outline of a Critical Theory of Ethics*, Register Publishing Co., Ann Harbor, 1891) and J. H. Tufts (*Ethics*, Henry Holt and Co., New York, 1932; *The Study of Ethics*, George Wahr Publishers, Ann Harbor, Michigan, 1897; *The Logical Conditions of a Scientific Treatment of Morality*, University of Chicago Press, Chicago, 1908; and *Theory of Valuation*, University of Chicago Press, Chicago, 1909). Of the Fourth *viz.*, the humanist type, are Warner Fite (*An Introductory Study of Ethics*, Longmans Green and Co., New York, 1906; *Moral Philosophy*, The Dial Press, New York, 1925; *Individualism*, Longmans, Green and Co., New York, 1924), C. 13. Garnett (*Wisdom in Conduct*, Harcourt Brace and Co., New York, 1940), Irving Babitt (*On Being Creative*, Houghton Mifflin Company, Boston, 1932), etc.
16. Examples of the first group are W. T. Stace (*The Concept of Morals*, The MacMillan Co., New York, 1937) Moritz Schlick (*Problems of Ethics*, tr. by David Rynin, Prentice Hall, New York, 1939); of the second group are George Santayana (*The Life of Reason or the Phases of Human Progress*, One Volume edition, Charles Scribner's Sons, New York, 1953, first published 1933; *Winds of Doctrine*, Charles Scribner's Sons, New York, 1926;

The Philosophy of George Santayana, Library of Living Philosophers, Evanston and Chicago, 1940, etc.), David Wright Prall (*A Study in the Theory of Value*, University of California Press, Berkeley, 1921; *The Present Status of Theory of Value*, University of California Press, Berkeley, 1923; *Naturalism and Norms*, University of California Press, Berkeley, 1925); of the third group are Ralph Barton Perry (*General Theory of Value*, Longmans, Green and Co., New York, 1926), Dewitt Henry Parker (*Human Values*, Harper and Brothers, New York, 1931), F. R. Tennant (*Philosophical Theology*, The University Press, Cambridge, 1928), etc.

17. Open Court Publishing Co., La Salle, Illinois, 1946.
18. Lewis, C. I., *Analysis of Knowledge and Valuation*, p. 365.
19. Ibid., p. 171.
20. Ibid., preface, p. viii.
21. Ibid., p. 400.
22. Ibid., pp. 404, 407.
23. Ibid.
24. Ibid., p. 375.
25. Ibid., p. 378.
26. Husserl, Edmund, *Ideas: General Introduction to Pure Phenomenology*, tr. by W. R. Boyce Gibson, George Allen and Unwin, Ltd., London, 1931, Second Impression, 1952, pp. 54-58.
27. Lewis C. I., *op. cit.*, p. 375. The symbolic logical representation of the principle is found in the same work, p. 230 *et seq*.
28. Hartmann, *Ethics*, Vol. I, pp. 183 ff., 234 ff., 241 ff., following Scheler and Husserl.
29. As far as is known to this author, C. I. Lewis published only one more work in ethics, besides his *Analysis*, *viz.*, *The Ground and Nature of the Right*, Columbia University Press, New York, 1955. Here Professor Lewis limited himself to a discussion of problems of deontology.
30. Hartmann, *Ethics*, Vol. I, pp. 247-297.
31. Ibid., pp. 341-343, "*Ethics or Theology.*"
32. According to Santayana, the essences are infinite in number and kind, and hover over the universe of being like cluster clouds of space particles. Furthermore, "an essence," he writes, "is an inert theme, something which cannot bring itself forward... The multitude of essences is absolutely infinite." (Santayana, George, *Realms of Being*, Charles Scribner's Sons, New

York, 1942, pp. 20-21).

33. Hartmann, *Ethics*, Vol. II, pp. 76 ff. "Now so far as the oppositions (*i.e.*, oppositions of moral determination) are genuine antinomies, the antagonism is between the values themselves. In themselves these antinomies are insoluble..." (Ibid., p. 77) "All conflicts among values are clashes of axiological determination as such. They would set a limit to the harmony even of a divinely perfect, of a world-ruling, providence and of reordination." (Ibid., Vol. I, pp. 301-302).

34. Ibid., Vol. I, pp. 217 ff.

35. See Vol. II of his *Ethics*, *cit. supra*, entitled *Moral Values*, and containing a highly instructive analysis of the principles governing the internal structure of the realm of values.

36. Scheler, Max, *op. cit.*, p. 262 fr. *Vom Ewigen im Menschen*, Neue Geist, Leipzig, 1923, pp. 274-276. For a critique of Scheler's position see Hartmann, *Ethics*, Vol. I, pp. 332-343; Vol. II, 27-29.

37. Niebuhr, Reinhold, *The Nature and Destiny of Man*, Vol. I, Charles Scribner's Sons, New York, 1943, pp. 162-165. Here Niebuhr misunderstood Scheler's notion of 'Geist,' as distinguished from discursive reason (the Greek *nous*) and by which Scheler meant the faculty through which we perceive values – "the primary consciousness of value" – as evidence for the Christian "idea of transcendence" (the self- and nature-transcending of man and his reach to a God-in whose image he is made). Tillich, Paul, *Systematic Theology*, Vol. I, The University of Chicago Press, 1951, pp. 43, 106-107. For Tillich, Scheler and the whole phenomenological school have rendered a good service in epistemology and ethics; but not in religion where the whole school stopped short of the truth because they failed to include an "existential-critical element" in their perspective. (Ibid., p. 107).

38. Hartmann, *Ethics*, Vol. III, p. 262.

39. Lewis C. I., *Analysis of Knowledge and Valuation*, pp. 387, 395-396, 432-434.

40. "Only the propositions of mathematics and empirical science have sense." (Carnap, Rudolph, *Philosophy and Logical Syntax*, Kegan Paul, London, 1935, p. 36).

41. Pap, Arthur, *Elements of Analytic Philosophy*, The MacMillan Co., New York, 1949, pp. 31-34; Von Mises, Richard, *Positivism: A Study in Human Understanding*, pp. 319-325; Stevenson, Charles L., *Ethics and Language*,

Yale University Press, New Haven, 1944, pp. 36 *et seq.*; Carnap, Rudolph, *The Unity of Science*, Kegan Paul, London, 1934, pp. 22 ff.

42. "If, now a philosopher says 'Beauty is good,' I may interpret him as meaning either 'Would that everybody loved the beautiful' – or 'I wish that everybody loved the beautiful.' – The first of these makes no assertion, but expresses a wish; since it affirms nothing, it is logically impossible that there should be evidence for or against it, or for it to possess either truth or falsehood. The second sentence, instead of being merely optative, does make a statement, but it is one about the philosopher's state of mind, it could only be refuted by evidence that he does not have the wish that he says he has. This second sentence does not belong to ethics, but to psychology or biography. The first sentence, which does belong to ethics expresses a desire for something, but asserts nothing." (Russell, Bertrand, *Religion and Science*, Thornton Butterworth, Ltd., London, pp. 236 ff.). Views identical to Russell's may be found in Ayer, A. J., *Language, Truth and Logic*, Oxford University Press, New York, 1936; Stevenson, Charles Leslie, *op. cit.*; Pap, Arthur, *op. cit.*; Schlick, Moritz, *Problems of Ethics*, tr. by D. Rynin, Prentice Hall, Inc., New York, 1939; etc.

43. Predominantly in *Religious Values*, The Abingdon Press, New York, 1925; *Moral Laws*, The Abingdon Press, New York, 1933; *Nature and Values*, Abingdon Cokesbury Press, New York, 1945; *Person and Reality: An Introduction to Metaphysics*, Ronald Press Co., New York, 1958; *Persons and Values*, Boston University Press, 1952.

44. *The Source of Human Good*, The University of Chicago Press, Chicago, 1946; *The Wrestle of Religion with Truth*, The MacMillan Co., New York, 1927; *Intellectual Foundation of the Faith*, Philosophical Library, 1961. "A Workable Idea of God," *Christian Century*, XLVI, Feb. 14, 1929, pp. 226-228; "God and Value," Chapter in *Religious Realism*, ed. D. C. Macintosh, The MacMillan Co., New York; "Values Primary Data for Religious Inquiry," *Journal of Religion, XVI*, 4, October, 1936, pp. 379-405; "Creative Freedom: Aim of Liberal Religion," *The Christian Register*, October, 1955. A discussion of Wieman's views by a number of Christian thinkers may be found in *The Empirical Theology of Henry Nelson Wieman*, Library of Living Theology, Vol. 4, The MacMillan Co., New York, 1963.

45. A full criticism of Perry's value theory by Brightman appeared as a chapter in E. C. Wilm's *Studies in Philosophy and Theology* (The Abingdon Press, New York, 1922, pp. 22-64) entitled "Neo-Realistic Theories of Value."

46. Brightman, E. S., *Religious Values*, pp. 123, 130.
47. Ibid., p. 126.
48. Ibid., p. 127.
49. Ibid., p. 136.
50. Sorley, William Ritchie, *Moral Values and the Idea of God*, The Gifford Lectures, 1915, The University Press, Cambridge, England, 1919.
51. Brightman, E. S., *Religious Values*, p. 169.
52. The problem of the dissertation, he wrote, is "to discover that organization of human interests which is most conducive to their maximum fulfillment" ("The Organization of Interests," Unpublished Ph.D. dissertation, Dpt. of Philosophy, Harvard University, 1917, p.1, quoted in Rich, Charles M., "Henry Nelson Wieman's Functional Theism as Transcending Event," Unpublished Ph. D. dissertation, School of Divinity, University of Chicago, 1962, p. 108).
53. Wieman, H. N., *The Wrestle of Religion with Truth*, The MacMillan Co., New York, 1927, p. 161.
54. "What we require is a *personal* integration (of interests) that shall be *socially qualified*, or that shall guarantee a harmonious fulfillment of all interests ... The highest good (is achieved when)... all persons are comprised within one community each member of which wills only what is consistent with the wills of all the rest." (Perry, FL B., *General Theory of Value*, Harvard University Press, Cambridge, 1954, p. 676-677).
55. Wieman, H. N.,"The Organization of Interests," Doctoral Dissertation *cit.*, pp. 194-195, quoted in Rich, Charles Mark, *op. cif.*, p. 152.
56. "Religion represents the utmost reach of human interest far surpassing its application to human society." (Wieman, "The Organization of Interests," p. 207; Rich, *op. cif.*, p. 153).
57. "Religion .., not only brings our experience of other persons into the process of creating a will, but it also takes in our total experience of nature ... When the cosmic purpose is my purpose ... then I experience continuous and complete satisfaction. This is that organization of interests for which we have been seeking throughout this investigation." (Wieman, ibid., p. 237; Rich, *op. cif.*, p. 159).
58. Wieman, ibid., p. 239; Rich, *op. cit.*, p. 162.
59. Wieman, ibid., p. 254; Rich, *op. cif.*, p. 169.
60. "I am convinced that religious inquiry is misdirected when some presence

pervading the total cosmos is sought to solve the religious problem. It is even more futile to search infinite being which transcends the totality of all existence. It is impossible to gain knowledge of the total cosmos. Consequently, beliefs about these matters are illusions ... What is true of science in this respect (*i.e.*, methodology) is true of philosophy and theology or any other way in which the human mind might attain knowledge ... Without sense experience there is no revelation of God ..." etc. (Wieman, "Intellectual Autobiography," in Bretall, *op. cit.*, pp. 4-5).

61. Wieman, "Reply to Meland," in Bretall, *op. cit.*, pp. 70-71.
62. Meland, B. E., "The Root and Form of Wieman's Thought," in Bretall, *op. cit.*, p. 56.
63. Ibid.
64. In his monumental *Al-Itqān fī ʿUlūm al-Qur'ān* (Al-Azhar Press, Cairo, 1318 A.H.), Jalāl al-Dīn al-Suyūṭī listed a large number of disciplines which, despite their apparent variety, all seek to establish that which, in the Qur'an, God intended to be the religiously, morally and aesthetically imperative, that which human desiring, willing and doing ought to aim at realizing. The discipline known as *asbāb al-nuzūl*, for instance, is said by al-Suyūṭī to bring about that "aspect of wisdom for the sake of which the revelation of a Qur'anic law was made" (Ibid., Vol. I, p. 29); to constitute "a firm road to the understanding of Qur'anic meanings" (Ibid.) and, quoting from Ibn Taymiyyah, "to bring a knowledge of that for the sake of which the revelation of the given verse was made by means of uncovering the immediate cause and circumstance of its revelation" (Ibid.); to enable us to derive the universal meaning-content, or moral, from the particular judgment of a unique, given case (Ibid., p. 31). Allowing for the fact of the absence of "value" as a contemporary philosophic notion, any reading of the table of contents of al-Suyūṭī's book of "sciences of the Qur'an," will expose the fact that these "sciences" are diverse attempts at uncovering the values of which the Qur'an is a conceptual expression.
65. Al-Suyūṭī went far beyond al-Wāḥidī who, in his famous classic, *Asbāb al-Nuzūl* (Hindiyyah Press, Cairo, 1316 A.H., p. 342) explained *Sūrah al-Fīl* (the chapter of the Elephant) purely historically. Al-Suyūṭī rightly saw that no *asbāb al-nuzūl* discussion of this surah is complete without uncovering the moral lessons it contains. (*Al-Itqān fī ʿUlūm al Qur'ān*, Vol. I, p. 32).
66. For a discussion of the view that the unity of God is equivalent to, and hence

convertible with, the unity of truth and value, see this author's *On Arabism*, Vol. I, *Urubah and Religion*, Djambatan, Amsterdam, 1962, pp. 12, 250 ff.

67. Shahrastānī, Muḥammad ibn ʿAbd al-Karīm al-, *Al-Milal wa al-Niḥal*, ed. by Muhammad Fathallah Badran, Al-Azhar Press, Cairo, 1328/1910, pp. 146, 176.

68. Ibid., p. 173.

69. Ibid., p. 146.

70. Ibid., p.174. Indeed, al-Shahrastānī recognized that the advocates of such views are the Jews "among whom anthropomorphism is a constantly recurring habit." (Ibid., p. 176).

71. Ibid., p. 29. We should not be misled, however by al-Shahrastānī's classification of Maʿbad and Ghaylān as founders of the Muʿtazilah sect, or authors of the first "deviation" from Islam, for he wrote from the perspective of a later time at which the deviations had loomed large on the horizons of Islamic thinking.

72. Ibid., p. 62.

73. Ibid., p. 65. al-Shahrastānī reports these words as coming from Wāṣil ibn ʿAṭā', student of al-Ḥasan al-Baṣrī and one of the elders of the Muʿtazilah movement.

74. Al-Ashʿarī, Abū al-Ḥasan ʿAlī ibn Ismāʿīl, *Maqālāt al-Islāmiyyīn wa Ikhtilāf al-Muṣallīn*, ed. by Muhammad Muhyi al-Din Abd al-Hamid, Vol. I, Maktabat al Nahḍah al-Miṣriyyah, Cairo, 1369/1950, p. 225.

75. Ibid.

76. Al-Shahrastānī, *op. cit.*, p. 135.

77. Ibid.

78. Ibid., p. 9.

79. Ibid. Jahm is reported to have argued as follows: "If God knew and then created, did His knowledge remain the same or not? If it remained the same, then in one respect (*viz.*, that of the new created thing) He was ignorant. For, that He knew that the thing is to be created is other than the knowledge that it has been created. On the other hand, if his knowledge did not remain the same, then it has changed; and that which changes is not eternal (uncreated or divine)." (Ibid.)

80. Al-Shahrastānī, *op. cit.*, p. 145 (Preface to the chapter on *Ṣifātiyyah*).

81. Ibid., p. 147.

82. Ibid. To ʿAbdullāh ibn Saʿīd, al-Shahrastānī adds the names of Abū al-ʿAbbās

al-Qalānisī and al-Ḥārith ibn Asad al-Muḥāsibī as co-inceptors of the science of *Kalām* and advocates of straightforward attributism.

83. Ibid., p. 145.
84. Ibid., p. 148.
85. Ibid., p. 152. Al-Ashʿarī, *op. cit.*, Vol. II, p. 202.
86. Al-Ghazālī, Abū Ḥāmid, *Iḥyā' ʿUlūm al-Dīn*, al-Maktabah al-Tijāriyyah al-Kubrā, Cairo, n.d., pp. 104-110.
87. Against the *Mushabbihah*, Al-Ghazālī wrote: "As it is rationally valid that God is actor without an organ of action (like hand, tongue, foot, body, tool, etc.) and knower without heart or brain, it is rational that He is seer without eye, hearer without ear... talker without words... *i.e.*, without sound or letter..." (Ibid., p. 109). Against the Muʿtazilī neutralizationists, he wrote: "God is knower with a knowledge, alive with a life, potent with a potency, wilier with a will, speaker with speech; hearer with hearing, seer with seeing, all of which attributes are eternal. Those who say, knower without knowing as the common saying says 'Rich without wealth, knowing without knowledge and knower without a thing known,' (are wrong); for knowledge, the knower and the known are as inseparable from one another ... and unimaginable in separation from one another as killing without the killer and the killed." (Ibid., p. 110).
88. Kant, Immanuel, *Critique of Pure Reason*, tr. by F. Max Muller, The MacMillan Co., New York, 1949, pp. 495 ff. ("Discovery and Explanation of the Dialectical Illusion in all Transcendental Proofs, of the Existence of a Necessary Being"), and p. 508 ff. ("Criticism of all Theology based on Speculative Principles of Reason").
89. Ibn Taymiyyah, T. D. A., *Bayān Muwāfaqat Ṣarīh al-Maʿqūl li Ṣaḥīḥ al-Manqūl*, on the margin of *Minhāj al-Sunnah al-Nabawiyyah fi Naqd Kalām al-Shīʿah wa al-Qadariyyah*, Al-Maṭbaʿah al-Kubrā al-Amīriyyah, Cairo, 1321, pp. 73-74.
90. Ibn Taymiyyah, T. D. A., *Minhāj al-Sunnah*, p. 241.
91. Ibid., *Majmūʿat al-Rasā'il al-Kubrā*, al-Maṭbaʿah al-Sharafiyyah, Cairo, 1323, Vol. I, p. 41; Vol. II, p. 34.
92. Ibn Taymiyyah, *Minhāj al-Sunnah*, Vol. I, p. 236.
93. Ibid., p. 237.
94. Ibid., p. 235.
95. Ibn Taymiyyah, *Majmūʿat al-Rasā'il al-Kubrā*, Vol. I, pp. 440, 465.

96. Arguing with Fakhr al-Dīn al-Rāzī, in this respect an advocate of strong Ashʿarī views, Ibn Taymiyyah wrote: "He says to us, You are not unitarians (*muwaḥḥidīn*) at all until you say God was and nothing else was. We answer, We do say God was and nothing else was. But if we say that God has always been endowed with all His attributes, are we not describing one God endowed with attributes? We gave them an example thereof, saying, Tell us about this date tree; does it not have a trunk, pinnate leaves, clusters of dioecious flowers... (etc.); does it not have a single name which was given to it as endowed with all these qualia? So is God ... endowed with all His attributes, still One and only One God?" (*Minhāj al Sunnah*, Vol. I, p. 234).
97. Whitehead, Alfred North, *Process and Reality*, Cambridge University Press, Cambridge, England, 1929, p. 433, where it is called "the fallacy of misplaced concreteness."
98. *Kitāb Jawāb Ahl al-Imān*, Maktabat al-Taqaddum, Cairo, 1322 A.H., pp. 1 ff.
99. *Muqaddimah fī Uṣūl al-Tafsīr*, al-Matḥaf al-ʿArabī, Damascus, 1936, pp. 7-8.
100. Ibn Taymiyyah's critique of sufism runs throughout all his works. The following, however, were devoted to it: *Ḥaqīqat Madhhab al-Ittiḥādiyyīn wa Waḥdat al-Wujūd wa Bayān Buṭlānihi bi al-Barāhīn al Naqliyyah wa al-ʿAqliyyah*, ed. by Rashid Rida, Al-Manar, Cairo, 1349 A.H., constituting Vol. IV of *Majmūʿat al-Rasā'il wa al-Masā'il al-Qayyimah*, pp. 61-120; *Kitāb Ibn Taymiyyah ilā Shaykh al-Ṣufiyyah*, pp. 161-183; *Fī Ṣifāt Allah wa ʿUluwwihi ʿan Khalqihi*, pp. 186-216. A summary of these views may be read in Abu Zahrah, Muhammad, *Ibn Taymiyyah, Ḥayātuhu wa ʿAṣruhu, Ārā'uhu wa Fiqhuhu*, Dār al Fikr al-ʿArabī, Second Edition, Cairo, 1958, pp. 326-339.

A Comparison of the Islamic and Christian Approaches to Hebrew Scripture

THIS ARTICLE ENDEAVORS to compare the Islamic and Christian approaches to Hebrew Scripture; that is to say, to describe the processes of thought implied in the transformation of Hebrew Scripture into the Old Testament and to compare them with those implied in the transformation of some narratives of Hebrew Scripture into the Qur'an. It does not seek to analyze the problem of literary or textual transmission, of how and when Hebrew Scripture became the Old Testament; or of where the Prophet Muhammad received his foreknowledge of Abraham, Jacob and Moses without which the Qur'anic revelations delivered by the angel would have been incomprehensible to him. Taking these questions for granted, it attempts to establish the significance of the Christianization and Islamization of Hebrew Scripture.

I

If we were to look upon Hebrew Scripture not as Old Testament or as Qur'an, but as Hebrew Scripture, and if we were to read it not in Victorian English or 20th Century American, but in the original Hebrew; if we were to allow Hebrew Scripture alone to speak for itself, to transport us to its own ancient world in Abraham's Ur, Jacob's Padan Aram, Moses' Egypt and Sinai, in Palestine and Persia and Assyria, if we were to allow Hebrew Scripture to place us, as it were, in the *Sitz-im-Leben* in which its poems, oracles and narratives were received as expressing the Hebrews' inner thoughts and feelings, fears and aspirations if indeed, we did all this and took full advantage of the achievements of biblical archaeology and ancient history, what would Hebrew Scripture appear in fact to be?

Read from this presupposition-free standpoint, Hebrew Scripture presents us with the story of the life of the Hebrew. Every theological and moral idea, historical or geographical account is subordinated to the overall theme of the growth and decay of a people, and derives its significance from its pertinence to the history of that people. Hebrew Scripture is the record of Hebrew national history, written and preserved for the sake of the Hebrews, in order to mirror or to inculcate their faith in themselves as a people or to edify them in that faith. It is often held that the most characteristic feature of this national history is their religion and that the most central concept of their religion is that of the Godhead. But the fact is that religion is a characteristic not of the Hebrews, but of their later descendants, the Jews. As we understand it today, religion was impossible to the Hebrews. Their "religion" was their nationalism; and it was this nationalism of the ancestors that became – with its literature, its laws and customs – the religion of later times, of the Exile and post-Exile Jews down to the present day. The Ancient Hebrew worshipped himself; he sang his own praise. His god, Jahweh, was a reflection of his own person, a genuine *deus ex machina* designed to play the role of other-self in the Hebrews' favorite intellectual game, viz., biographical painting or self-portraiture in words.

The god of the Hebrews is not what Christians and Muslims understand by the word "God," or what modern Jews understand by that term after centuries of exposure to Christian and Islamic influences. Rather, the "God" of the Hebrews is a deity which belonged to the Hebrews alone. They worshipped it as "their God," always calling it by its own proper names, of which it had many. To be sure that it is not confused with any other gods – the possibility and existence of which was never denied, though they were always denigrated – the Hebrews were fond of calling their god by the unmistakably relational names of "God of Abraham, ... of Jacob, ... of Isaac, ... of Israel, ... of Zion," etc.[1] This deity could not even conceive of itself as capable of being worshipped outside the limits of their geographic domain.[2] Their mind was so obsessed with "the God of the Hebrews" that it was incapable of developing the concept "God" as a connotative category of thought rather than a class name with denotative meaning only. Theirs was certainly not monotheism, but monolatry, since there is not a single time where such a connotative concept of God occurs in Hebrew Scripture. Wherever "God" is mentioned, it is always the particular deity that is in question.[3] True, at a late stage of their history and only at that stage, they did regard their god as lord of the universe, but their doing so was always an attempt at extending its jurisdiction so as to requite their own national enemies. Their god was never the god of the *goyim* in the sense in which he was said to be the god of the Hebrews; the former always falling under his power in sufferance, as patients of his might, especially of his revenge of his people, never equally as subjects of his own creation or care.[4] Significantly, such extension of his jurisdiction did not take place except under the dream of Isaiah of a master-race, vanquishing the nations and entering them into a relation of servile servitude to the Hebrews.[5]

II

This Hebrew Scripture was Christianized. Its Christianization appears to have been predetermined by four notions which are implications of the Christian belief that Jesus is God. These pertain to the nature of revelation, the nature of divine action, the nature of man and the nature of God.

First, the Christian believes that Jesus is "the Word of God." This fact determines for him the nature of revelation. Since Jesus was also man, and therefore an event in history, divine revelation must be an event; not something that God says, but something that He does. And Jesus is the revealed word inasmuch as he is a doing of God, a historical event, whose every part or deed is divine because Jesus himself is wholly God. From this it follows that revelation is not ideational but personal and historical.[6] Jesus, the perfect personality, the perfect event, the perfect history, is according to this belief, God's perfect revelation.

From this Christian point of view, Hebrew Scripture is not the conceptual word of God, but that of the Jahwist, Elohist, Deuteronomist and Priestly editors. Its divine status does not pertain to its ideas and laws. These constitute the human tools which the editors have used in order to record the revelation. The word of God in Hebrew Scripture is the events, the doing and living of Hebrew Scriptural personalities. These events *are* revelation. Pointing to the dramas of Hebrew Scripture, the Christian exclaims, *Voila* God's acts in history! Acts all designed and predetermined by Him to the end that He may reveal Himself and achieve His purpose. God's method being that of revelation through personality, God chose a people, the Hebrews, and took them by the hand, as it were, on a long journey. At the end of this journey, when the time was fulfilled, He sent His Word, Jesus, and through his personality, *i. e.*, his living and dying, God achieved man's redemption. Hebrew history is *Heilsgeschichte* or salvation-history.

This position has advantages: It provides what is for Christians the greatest event of history, *viz.* the advent of Jesus, with the necessary anticipatory set of historical events, the antecedent links in a determined nexus of historical events. It gives a theological sense to Hebrew national life, to the Jews' self-centeredness and separatism; for under its purview, their self-centeredness is not racialist nationalism but something which subserves a divine purpose. Finally, the words and, indeed, even the individual deeds of scriptural personalities can be as banal or as sublime as they may. The divine element that is here involved is the broad-stepping movement of history, the constituents of which are the more significant events of election, migration, exodus, invasion and conquest, political growth and decay, defeat and exile as well as the response of faith and trust, the handing down of the law, the dawning of the Messiah-expectancy, etc.

This position of the Christian presents a few difficulties, however. It runs counter to the textual evidence of "Thus saith the Lord." The prophets had a sincere and arresting consciousness that the word they spoke was dictated to them by their God. Under the Christian view, "Thus saith the Lord" must be explained psychologically; for God acts, rather than speaks. And if on the other hand, God were to reveal Himself once by acting and once by speaking, the question then becomes one of assigning primacy to either form of communication. The Christian, if he is to speak as a Christian, must uphold the preeminence of event above all else. Indeed he must hold all speech-revelation as subservient to and determined by event-revelation. Thus, *Koh amar Yahweh* ["Thus saith Yahweh"] may have been sincerely uttered by the prophets, but it was not really true. They were under illusion. The truth is that God merely caused them to see it that way; but it was not really, absolutely, so.

Secondly, the notion of a deterministic history, though the kind of determination that is here in question does not have to be the efficient, the material or the formal, but the finalistic, is not easily reconciled with the ethical facts, the phenomena of freedom, of responsibility and of conscience. There is little evidence to support the thesis that Jacob's migration to Egypt was an act of God and not the free responsible act of Jacob; that the successful escape of the Hebrews from Egypt and their victory over the Canaanites were not of their own doing. Historical determinism, even though the determiner is God, is groundless speculative construction. At best, it is a theory; a theory contradicted by moral phenomena, the *facts* of ethical living and acting. It is an instance of the logical fallacy known under the name of *simplex sigillum veri*, in this case, the acceptance of a finalistic explanation of an event because it is the simplest; because the finalistic explanation satisfies a longing engendered by the primacy of finalistic considerations for man; because, lastly, man tends to explain everything in his own image, as if that thing were human. This, however, is the fallacy of groundless extrapolation. For historical determinism extrapolates the finalistic explanation from the realm of human biography where it properly belongs, to that of cosmic history where human purposiveness is ruled out by definition. It remains a fact, however – and we acknowledge it readily – that nature and cosmos appear *as if* purposiveness is true of their unfolding in history. But this feature is never constitutive and may never be critically established. It remains a mere "*als ob*."

In Islam, revelation is ideational and only ideational. "Thus saith the Lord" is the only form revelation can take. Islam upholds the prophetic notion of immediate and direct revelation as given in Hebrew Scripture. "Thus saith the Lord" means precisely what it says. For, in Islam, God does not reveal Himself. Being transcedent, He can never become the object of knowledge. But he can and does reveal His will; and this is wholly the ethically-imperative, the commandment, the law. This He reveals in the only way possible for revealing the law, namely, the discursive word. The moral law is a conceptually-communicable, ideational schema of a value-content endowed with moving appeal. Certainly, it is not an event. The event may or may not realize the moral law; but it is not itself the law.

This Islamic view of revelation, which is also that of Hebrew Scripture, does not conflict with the phenomena of responsibility, freedom and conscience. For an idea does not coerce. It "moves;" and man may very well be, as not-be, "moved" by the idea. An event, on the contrary is one necessarily caused by necessary causes and issuing in necessary effects. Islam therefore is safe against ever having to rely upon a deterministic theory of history in order to justify itself. It does hold, though, that God may act in history. But such a divine act it always interprets as the reward of virtue or the punishment of vice; and it explains such divine intervention in history as the necessary real connection, or causal bond, that relates the real-existential *matériaux* of moral value or disvalue, with those of happiness or suffering. The so-called "saving acts of God" in Hebrew Scripture, Islam regards as the natural consequences of virtue and good deeds.

The notion that revelation is by event, which follows from the notions that Jesus, the "God-man in history," is both "the Word of God" and himself the revelation of God, further determines the Christian understanding of Hebrew election and covenant. For the Christian, Abraham's election is God's call to faith and his response is the predetermined response of faith. The patriarchal Chosen-People-complex he understands as the fact that the Hebrews suffered themselves to be the tools of God's acts. Their insistence that they are a race chosen by God absolutely, i.e., for its own sake and for all time – a race chosen to be the favorite not as a reward for some virtue or worth but for its own sake – is understood by the Christian as God's faithfulness in keeping his term of the covenant, and the elect's faithfulness in being the recipient of God's election; as his insistence "on maintaining his part of the Covenant," as one of the foremost biblical scholars puts it, "even when Israel had broken that Covenant."[7] If you, Hosea, cannot put away your wife, though unfaithful and guilty, how can I, Jahweh, put away my people, though they are unrighteous and a stiff-necked people?[8] Indeed, they are and shall remain my chosen favorites no matter what they do. This Hebrew callousness to the moral truth that only the more virtuous may be said to be the worthier, is offensive to moral sense. Hence, the Christian does try to 'ethicize' it, as when he holds it to be an election to the onerous burden of being the messengers of God. But this rationalization falls to the ground when we consider the doctrine of the remnant – equally biblical – which asserts that the Hebrews would remain the elect even when they have stopped "messengering," when they have stopped being and acting as God's ambassadors to men. But just as we may not hold election to be a matter of merit when the subject has become unworthy, we may not hold that election is a matter of embassy when the subject no more acts in that capacity.[9]

The covenant is a perfectly ethical notion if only all it purports to say is the truth that if man obeys God and does the good, he would be blessed. As such, it is the Semitic way of saying that virtue = happiness. It lays upon man an obligation – that of obeying God, of doing the good, and upon God an expectation, if not an equally binding obligation, that whoever obeys God and does the good will be blessed and happy. Although there is plenty of talk of "the Covenant," yet the Hebrew Scripture covenant is nothing of the sort. It is, more properly, a promise, a one-directional favor-proffering by God upon "His people." This transformation of the covenant into "the Promise" is the other side of the racialization of election.

The Qur'an admits that God had sent His word to the Hebrews, and that many a prophet and many a man believed and did rightly, and were consequently "blessed" and "raised above the rest."[10] But the rest rejected God's word and were hence subject to his dire punishment.[11] For the covenant is a purely ethical contract, unequivocally binding upon man and God.[12] It is not denied.[13] "Allah accepted a [similar] solemn pledge from the children of Israel ... And God said: 'Behold, I shall be with you! If you are constant in prayer, and spend in charity, and believe in My apostles and aid them, and offer up unto God a goodly loan, I will surely efface your bad deeds and bring you into gardens through which running waters flow.'"[14] The Qur'an also awards the status of elect to the Muslims,[15] but on the firm basis that the Hebrews had rejected the prophets, the messengers of God, including Jesus; and with the unequivocal understanding that God's word is a command to be realized, that if the Muslims should ever fail to fulfil that command, God will not only withdraw the trust and the election, but would destroy them and give their property as inheritance to another people more prepared to carry it out.[16]

It is true that in extending election from Israel to the New Israel, the Christian divests it of its Hebraic racialism and transforms it into an election by faith, and this transformation stands at the root of his doctrine of justification by faith (Rom. 4, Gal. 3). In Islam, election and justification are not at all by faith, but by works. Faith in Islam is only a condition, valuable and often necessary, but not indispensable. The Qur'an counts among the saved not only the *ḥanīfs*, or the pre-Islamic righteous, but many post-Islamic Christians and Jews and gives as reason for their salvation their devoted worship of God, their humility, their charity and their good deeds.[17] Islam may be said to have recaptured the pure Semitic vision, beclouded by the old Hebrew racialism as well as by the new 'Christianism,' of a moral order of the universe in which every human being, regardless of his race or color – indeed of his religion in the institutionalized sense – gets exactly what he deserves, only what his works and deeds earn for him on an absolute moral scale of justice. Certainly God may award His compassion, love and mercy to whomsoever He pleases; but it is not for man to go about the world carrying his title to paradise, as it were, in his pocket.

The desperate attempt of Christian doctrine to save ethics from the sure death to which justification by faith leads it by requiring man to live the life of gratitude, i.e. of one whom God has irrevocably saved, exposes morality to the fanaticism implicit in a monistic axiology, where the value of gratitude is the only value, or to the implicit vacuity – where gratitude can mean all, any member or none of the whole realm of values, as each individual decides for himself in Protagorean relativist fashion, or the community decides for him by convention. On the other hand the denial that God's salvation is irrevocable opens the Christian faith to the charge that salvation is not a completed historical event, but an ideational command – whether carried by the discursive word or the exemplary deed – which is granted or denied as each person fulfils or fails to fulfil the morally imperative.

Islam, therefore, approaches Hebrew Scripture with the absolute moral law as the only presupposition; and it starts right at the beginning of the Hebrew and Christian tale of election and promise. Against the arbitrary, uncaused, unjustified "Get thee out" of Genesis 12, which marks the beginning of Hebrew racialist election, it explains the departure of Abraham from his people and land as the regrettable result of his dispute over their idolatry. Even so, the separation was temporary and Abraham is described as praying for his father and people that God may rightly guide them. The so-called "Legends of Abraham," – his destruction of the idols, his being visited by angels, his redemption from the burning fire of Nimrod – all these come only from the Qur'an, the earliest appearance of them outside Islam being the Codex Sylvester of the *Ma'am Abraham* which a Russian monk picked up in a thirteenth century bazaar in Constantinople, and the more recent *Midrash Hagadol*, written in the Seventeenth Century and discovered in Yemen in the nineteenth.[18]

III

If there is to be a redeeming, evidently there must be something from which man is to be redeemed; and secondly, this something must be such that man cannot redeem himself from it by his own agency. This something must be universal and necessary; and this is precisely what Christian "sin" is. Looking into Hebrew Scripture, the Christian discerns this universal and necessary sin in Adam.

The Christian takes Adam's disobedience to be the real and actual sin of mankind. Adam's tasting of the tree of knowledge of good and evil is declared to be man's necessary will to assert himself, to have his own way; man's knowing, to be his pride and confidence in his own capacity. The Hebrews did not understand Adam's story in this manner; and the Christian has therefore found it necessary to transfigure Adam's disobedience into "sin." The obligation to work and to suffer pain is hedonistically understood to mean doom and death eternal. Adam's misdemeanor is universalized as that of the whole human race.

The Christian respect for personality, with its implied personalist theory of truth, should have prescribed that the sin of Adam be the sin of Adam alone. If, on the other hand, Adam is only a symbolic figure, it is nothing but the barest assertion to claim that sin is the necessary and universal phenomenon, that it is the starting point of man's career on earth. Virtue is no less a universal phenomenon; and if it were to provide that starting point, an outlook totally different from that of Christianity would follow. Nonetheless, this Christian emphasis on sin is not without merit. Undoubtedly, sin is more often the rule than virtue. In the matter of man's career on earth, the career of ever transcending himself in emulation of the divine, his shortcoming is far more relevant than his advantage. In battle, the enemy should occupy a peculiar category in the consciousness of general and soldier. The Christian's obsession with sin is not altogether unhealthy and has the merit of focusing attention on that which is to be overcome. But this advantage immediately turns sour if attention to sin is exaggerated, as is the case with Christian doctrine, where it becomes the first principle of creation as well as of man's moral being. However, the Christian asserts sin in order to deny it; for the Jesus-event had no rationale save the destruction of sin as a universal and primordial phenomenon, as human essence. But having denied it in the assertion that universal salvation is a *fait accompli*, the Christian has *ipso facto* forfeited his moral enthusiasm and laid wide open the gates of moral complacency. Gratitude, or the recognition that God has in fact saved him, gives man no ethic other than the obligation to give thanks and proclaim the salvation-news. That is precisely how many Christians (e.g. Karl Barth) understand the moral imperative. Faced with such difficulties, the Christians interpret Adam's act in a variety of ways: Some insist that it is his knowledge of good and evil; others, that it is his desire to be like God; others, that it is his self-assertion and egotism; others more philosophic but with no little Buddhistic sensitivity and existential boredom with life, that it is his very actuality and existence.[19] All these views evidently imply either that man's creation was faulty or that it was undesirable. They transform man's noblest endowments, *viz.* – his knowledge and will to knowledge, his cosmic uniqueness, his will to be and to persist, his will to become like unto God, into instruments of doom.

In Islam, far from being the father of sin, Adam is the father of the prophets. He received his learning directly from God, and in this he was superior to the angels to whom he taught the "names" (i.e. essences, definitions) of the creatures.[20] God commanded him to pursue the good[21] as well as to avoid evil, the latter being the nature of the tree whose fruit he was forbidden to eat. The identification of the tree as "the tree of life and knowledge" is neither God's nor Adam's; but, if a Muslim may here make a guess on the basis of Christian Old Testament scholarship, the work of the priestly editors of "J" who branded knowledge of good and evil as evil in pursuit of their will to power and in perpetration of their monopoly over man's reaching toward God. The Qur'an calls this wrong identification a lie told by Satan in order to lure Adam, prone as he was to know and pursue the good, to transgress God's command and do evil. "Satan," the Qur'an says, "whispered unto him, saying: 'O Adam! Shall I lead thee to the tree of life eternal; and [thus] to a kingdom that will never decay?' And so the two ate [of the fruit] thereof: and thereupon they became conscious of their nakedness and began to cover themselves with pieced-together leaves from the garden. And [thus] did Adam disobey his Sustainer, and thus did he fall into grievous error. Thereafter, [however,) his Sustainer elected him [for His grace], and accepted his repentance, and bestowed His guidance upon him."[22] Adam, therefore, did commit a misdeed, *viz.*, that of thinking evil to be good, of ethical misjudgment. He was the author of the first human mistake in ethical perception, committed, with good intention, under enthusiasm for the good.[23] It was not a "fall" but a discovery that it is possible to confuse the good with the evil, that its pursuit is neither unilateral nor straightforward.

The fact that Jesus has redeemed man not only implies a theory of man – which we have just discussed, – but equally a theory of God. Jesus, for the Christian, *is* God; and redemption not only implies a certain kind of man, but equally a certain kind of God; a God who is so concerned about man that He would redeem him by doing what Jesus did, or by doing what He did 'in' Jesus.

Thus, the Christian looks upon the declaration of Genesis, "Let us make man according to our image" and sees therein the confirmation he needs of man's fellowship with God. Man, an image of God, was created to be God's fellow in paradise. But man has sinned. God would not acquiesce in this estrangement, in this self-waste to which man has committed himself. Hence, he punished him at first; then he chased him out of paradise and inflicted upon him all sorts of afflictions. Nonetheless man continued to sin. God then decided that all creation was a mistake except for one man, Noah, and his family, and destroyed all life in a Deluge. Thereafter, touched by the "sweet savor" of Noah's sacrifice, God vowed never to destroy life again as He had just done. But man continued to sin. Whereupon God decided upon another course of action, the election of the Hebrews and their divinely-operated history to the end that he may himself assume man's sin and redeem him, acting through the God-man Jesus. All this points to the fact that God is man's partner and fellow, and man is God's partner and fellow, each of whom is indispensable for the other.

This Christian fellowship of man with God, though drawn from a Hebrew Scriptural account, puts God in a position irreconcilable with his omniscience and omnipotence. Nonetheless, it contains a great deal of truth. For despite the context in which the Christian understands it, man's "fellowship" with God is an expression of the rapport which exists between God's commandment, the ethically imperative, or value, and man. This rapport consists in that the ought-to-be, the modality of the ideally-existent value which possesses genuine moving power and being, is beamed towards man. It also consists in the capacity of the latter alone in creation to grasp that ought-beam and fall under its determination. Man's capacity to know and to do the good, or God's will, is his "divinity." God's moving power, directed to man, is his "humanity." But it should not be forgotten that this "human divinity" and "divine humanity" are not real facts, but mere modalities of real facts. The ought-to-be is a necessary modality of value; it may not be called a "need" unless value, or divinity, is hopelessly anthropomorphic; and it is crude to speak of it as a "fellowship," or to ascribe to it the assumption of man's "guilt," to "crucify" it, etc. which the Christian does.

In Islam, God created man for the specific purpose of carrying out a trust in this world, a trust so great that the angels, to whom it was first offered, turned away in terror.[24] This trust is the perfecting of an imperfect world deliberately created imperfect so that in the process of a human perfecting of it, ethical values would be realized which otherwise (i.e., in a necessarily perfectible or created-perfect world) would be ruled out *ex hypothesi*. God, therefore, is not man's fellow, but his Transcendent Creator and First Mover whose moving does stand *en rapport* with man's capacity for being moved. The nearness of a First Mover, of value as a genuine entelechy, is beyond question. But it is not the nearness of a "fellow" who is willing to do his partner's supreme duty, as in Christianity. Rather, it is the nearness of a modality of our knowledge of the being of the Godhead, the nearness of the ethically imperative.

IV

In conclusion, we may therefore say that the Christian approach to Hebrew Scripture is dogmatic; i.e., governed by the desire to confirm articles of the Christian creed; whereas the Islamic approach is ethical, i.e., governed by absolute and immutable ethical laws, without regard to dogma. In consequence of his approach being dogmatic, the Christian is compelled to resort to a deterministic view of man and history, to an allegorical interpretation of unequivocal texts and to glossing over accounts and narratives of human conduct which no worthy morality can accept. *Per contra*, in consequence of his approach being ethical, the Muslim is compelled to separate the ethically valid from the perverse in Hebrew Scripture, for only the former he can call the Word of God. But Hebrew Scripture does not lose by having any of its parts demoted, as it were, from the status of revelation to that of human editing. Unlike revelation, human writing is capable of having both the good and the evil. On the contrary, rather than losing, Hebrew Scripture gains through such an attitude. Such an attitude to Hebrew Scripture as the Qur'an expresses is the first pre-requisite of the whole discipline known as Old Testament criticism which has saved Hebrew Scripture from the slow but sure process of repudiation by Christians of the last two centuries, by correcting its claims, reconciling its contradictions, and reconstructing its history on a sounder foundation. The first principle of this discipline has been the Qur'anic principle that not all the Old Testament is God's word, but only some; that much of it – Christian scholars go to the extreme of claiming that all of it – is the work of editors and redactors of all sorts of affiliation.

Furthermore, because of his approach, the Christian is faced with the insurmountable problem of the *Vergegenwärtigung* (i.e. the representation or making contemporary and relevant) of Hebrew Scripture, of the Old Testament. For being a revelation in events, the relevance of past events for the present may always be put to question. The Islamic approach, which reads in Hebrew Scripture immutable though often violated ethical principles, and in Hebrew history some violation as well as some fulfilment of these principles, stands in no need of such *Vergegenwärtigung*. Ethical principles are always contemporary. But for the Christian, the problem is so great that nobody has so far given a satisfactory answer, while the Christian masses become ever more and more alienated from Hebrew Scripture. Indeed, *Vergegenwärti-*

gung is such an insoluble problem that men of the caliber of G. von Rad,[25] Karl Barth[26] and Martin Noth[27] have spoken of a solution by proclamation. We may "vergegenwärtigen" the Old Testament, they tell us, by proclaiming its news, its events, "just as we would read a sheaf of news reports and pass them on just as they are."[28] 'Proclaim the Old Testament as you please,' a friendly warner may say in this connection, 'the masses of Christendom will continue to give you an unsilenceable retort: So what?'

Notes

1. W. F. Albright has noted that the Hebrews conceived of their god as if he were their relative, and they were his brothers, uncles, nephews and kinsmen; that no such relationship was possible for any person that did not already belong to their order (*From the Stone Age to Christianity*, Johns Hopkins Press, Baltimore, 1940, pp. 185 ff.).
2. I. Samuel 26:19; II Kings 5:17.
3. See the informative discussion in *Encyclopaedia Biblica*, *s. v.* Names, Divine Names.
4. Against this it is often contended that the Old Testament does contain evidence of a universalist divine providence in the Book of Jonah, in Amos 9, Isaiah 15 and 19. However, a careful reading of the Book of Jonah reveals that the significance of the story does not lie in what God did to Nineveh but in the Jewish attitude to Nineveh represented not only by the man-in-the-street but by no less a man than the "prophet" Jonah himself. In Amos 9:7 it is claimed that God has done as much *for* Israel as he did *for* the Philistines and the Syrians – a wrong and perverse opinion. It is wrong because rather than emphasize what God did to the non-Jews, the whole purport of verse 7 as well as the first half of chapter 9, is to show that Jahweh is mighty enough to destroy Israel. As evidence of this divine might the Old Testament cites what Jahweh did to the non-Jews. Finally, Isaiah's "Blessed be Egypt, My people, and Assyria, the work of My hands," cannot be taken seriously. The Egypt and Assyria which are here blessed had been totally destroyed (Isaiah 19:1 ff.) lost their spirit and purpose (ibid., 19:3, 10), changed their spirit for a "perverse" one (ibid., 19:4) and become "the city of destruction unto whom the land of Judah shall be a terror" (ibid., 19:17). Furthermore they had been repopulated by Israelites (ibid., 19:4-10) changed their language for that of Canaan, and now cooperate together in the service of an imperial Israel (ibid., 19:23-24). It takes a logic quite unique to make white out of this Isaiahn jet-black.

5. Isaiah 49:22-23. For the Jews, Hebrew Scripture is the yet-unfinished record of Hebrew history.
6. "God... can only reveal Himself perfectly in perfect personality ... (and) ... The word of God is mediated to us through the instrument of their (the redactors of Hebrew Scripture) personality" Rowley, H. H. *The Relevance of the Bible*, London: J. Clarke & Co., 1941, p. 25.
7. Frost, S. B., *The Beginning of the Promise*, London: SPCK, 1960, p. 46; Snaith, Norman, *The Distinctive Ideas of the Old Testament*, London: The Epworth Press, 1944, eighth impression, 1960, p. 140.
8. Hosea 1:10; 11:8-9; 13:14. The Jews understand by Deuteronomy, 14:1, that even when the children's conduct is unfilial, the filial relation remains (and) "sinful offspring are still children (of God)" (*Universal Jewish Encyclopaedia*, New York, 1941, Vol. III, p. 167, quoting R. Meir). Also, R. Johanan commented thus on Hosea's inability to repudiate his prostitute-wife despite her misconduct: "If you [God must have argued with Hosea] cannot put away your wife of whose fidelity you are uncertain ... how can I reject Israel who are my children?..." (ibid., p. 168). In an argument of unparalleled intellectual bravado, Th. C. Vriezen distinguishes an "empirical Israel" from what he presumably takes to be an absolute or transcendental Israel. "Even if God rejects the empirical Israel in its entirety for some time," he writes "that does not mean that Israel is rejected altogether ... Israel was never rejected absolutely ... This implies the continuous faithfulness of the electing God rather than the possibility of definite rejection by God of what He has once elected... As far as Israel is concerned rejection only exists partially and temporarily as punishment. Cf. my *Die Erwahlurzg Israels*, pp. 98 ff." (*An Outline of Old Testament Theology*, Oxford: B. Blackwell, 1958, p. 142). Walter Eichrodt is so convinced of the absoluteness of Israel's election that he takes the Hosean passage in question as evidence that the Old Testament God is no capricious despot "striking out in blind rage," as if for Him to reject Israel when she broke the covenant, would have been tantamount to "acting in blind rage." (*Theology of the Old Testament*, Vol. I, London: SCM Press, 1960, p. 265).
9. For a further discussion of this view *see* this author's review of Frost, S. B., *op. cit.*, in *Christian Outlook*, Montreal, No. 1960.
10. Qur'an, 2:47; 7:168.
11. Ibid., 7:100-102.

12. Ibid., 2:40.
13. Ibid., 2:63, 84; 3:187; 5:70; 7:172.
14. Ibid., 5:12.
15. Ibid., 3:104, 110.
16. Ibid., 47:38; 9:39.
17. "And, behold, among the followers of earlier revelation there are indeed such as [truly] believe in God, and in that which has been bestowed from on high upon you as well as in that which has been bestowed upon them. Standing in awe of God, they do not barter away God's messages for a trifling gain. They shall have their reward with their Sustainer – for, behold, God is swift in reckoning!" (Qur'an, 3:199; see also ibid., 2:162).
18. It was in the 11th century that Hebrew literature acquired a great mass of material from Arabic sources. Nissim of Kairawan, author of the famous *Sefer Ma'asoth*, combined stories from the Haggadah, the Bidpai Fables which he took over complete in their Arabic title of "Kalīlah wa Dimnah," with Qur'anic narratives, *A Thousand and One Nights* stories, etc. Nonetheless, the *Sefer Ma'asoth* does not even have a *Ma'ase Abraham*, which must have been a later addition.
19. An example of the last instance is the case of Paul Tillich who understands the fall as "transition from essence to existence" but upholds the Christian prejudice that such transition is unworthy and condemnable in order to make room for salvation (*Systematic Theology*, Vol. II, Chicago: University of Chicago Press, 1957, pp. 29-31). When finally salvation did come through Jesus, it did not transform man back into essence, but merely taught him to regard existence no more as condemnable. True, existence as "estrangement" had its marks (sin, *hubris*, concupiscence) which, Jesus had shown, could be surmounted (Ibid., pp. 125-6). Nonetheless, the saved man is not one standing outside existence, but in existence surmounting its antinomies and disvalues (Ibid., pp. 16 ff.). But in this case, the definition of the fall as transition from essence to existence has availed nothing.
20. Qur'an, 2:30-32. The Qur'an does not read in Hebrew history any history-determinism. The so-called saving acts of God, and above all, the Exodus with all its surrounding mystery, are all there. But they are acts of God only inasmuch as they are the natural consequences of virtue and good deeds. All these are metaphorically called the rewards of those who remained steadfast in their worship and service of God and were persecuted and exploited

by a tyrant Pharaoh. The blessing of Abraham with children and land, the Exodus and subsequent guidance and blessing of the Hebrews in Sinai and their entry into possession of Palestine were, according to the Qur'an, not part of an operated history, but God's part of the covenant, the blessing or happiness which is the necessary consequence of virtue. The same justification is applied by the Qur'an to David's victory over Goliath, as well as to the glories of Solomon's reign. In no case does the Qur'an compromise the freedom or responsibility of these men by implying a divine operation of the historical nexus (Qur'an, 73:15; 28:3 ff.; 20:77-83; etc.). What is forgotten here is that while an idea may be caused to appear, as the notion of "*Koh amar Jahweh*" proves, it is of its very nature not to determine the addressee, whose doings remain his own choice and responsibility. "Thus saith the Lord" can never imply a historical determinism such as Hebrew history is here claimed to be. Once more, the difference between Christianity and Islam is precisely this, that in the former, revelation is an event, in the latter, it is an idea. The former sees in Hebrew history a series of revelation-events which could not have not-happened (a God-authored event is by definition something necessarily causing necessary effects and is necessarily caused by necessary causes) and the latter, a series of revelation ideas which were freely accepted by some and freely rejected by others. The "Promise" of Hebrew Scripture, or the unearned blessing of any man or people, the Qur'an utterly rejects as inconsonant with God's nature and His justice; the Muslims being no more unfit for such favoritism than any other people.

21. Ibid., 20:116-9.
22. Ibid., 20:120-122.
23. Hence, God's admonition to Adam: "You (Satan and Adam) shall leave paradise, enemies one to the other, until guidance (i.e. the guarantee against perceptual errors in matters ethical) comes to you from me" (ibid., 20: 123-4).
24. Ibid., 33:72.
25. Von Rad, G., *Das Fornigeschichtliche Problem des Hexateuchs*, (BWANT 26), Stuttgart, 1938, pp. 18 *ff.*
26. Barth, Karl, "Das Christliche Verständnis der Offenbarung," in *Theologische Existenz Heute*, 12, 1948, pp. 9, 13 ff., quoted by Martin Noth, *in op. cit., infra*, note 27.
27. Noth, Martin, "Interpretation of the Old Testament, I. The 'Re-presenta-

tion' of the Old Testament in Proclamation," *Interpretation*, January, 1961, pp. 50-60. In this article Noth reviews the history of the problem and discusses the views of Karl Barth as well as G. Von Rad.

28. The words are Karl Barth's, cited by Noth, *loc. cit.*

History of Religions: Its Nature and Significance for Christian Education and the Muslim-Christian Dialogue[1]

I
THE NATURE OF HISTORY OF RELIGIONS

HISTORY OF RELIGIONS is an academic pursuit composed of three disciplines: Reportage, or the collection of data; Construction of meaning-wholes, or the systematization of data; and Judgement, or Evaluation, of meaning-wholes.[2]

1. *Reportage, or the Collection of Data*

History of religions has known two influences which sought to reduce its jurisdiction by limiting the data which constitute its subject matter: One was the attempt to redefine the religious datum in a restricted and narrow manner; and the other was an isolationist policy observed *vis-a-vis* Judaism, Christianity and Islam.

A. The attempt to limit the jurisdiction of history of religions by giving the religious datum a narrow definition developed theories which have tried to isolate the religious element and to identify it in terms of "the religious," "the holy," "the sacred." The problem these theories faced was primarily the reductionist's analysis of the religious phenomenon into something else that lends itself more readily to his kind of investigation. On the history of religions, this well-intended movement had the effect of limiting the scope of the investigation. If the religious is a unique, irreducible and identifiable element in human life, the religious discipline should aim at it first and last. The other elements of which human life is supposedly composed may be the objects of other disciplines and they may be studied by the history of religions only as *relata* affecting or affected by the uniquely religious element. Among historians of religions in the West, where the act of faith has been held to consist in the confrontation of the person with God in his most personal moment when everything or almost everything that is non-self has been detached from consciousness, the discovery of "the religious" as a unique element fell on fertile ears and was taken as a matter of course.[3] Today, fortunately, the relevance of God to every aspect and element of space-time is being rediscovered by Western Christendom, and the repudiation of an isolated unique religious holy or sacred is being prepared for. In its place, the religiousness of everything is being discovered, a religiousness which does not consist in the thing's being a mere relatum. For a century the Christian theologian has been talking of the whole act of the person as social and not merely of his personal act, as constitutive of the religious; and more recently, of a Christian "style of living" in an attempt to sacralize the whole of life. Islam has for centuries been teaching the religiousness of all space-time, of all life.

Not only the personal act of faith, nor the social act, nor the whole of space-time and life as relata, but the whole of life and space-time as such constitute the data of history of religions. History of religions studies every human act because every act is an integral part of the religious complexus. Religion itself, however, is not an act (the act of faith, or encounter with God, or of participation), but a dimension of every act. It is not a thing; but a perspective with which every thing is invested. It is the highest and most important dimension; for it alone takes cognizance of the act as personal, as standing within the religio-cultural context in which it has taken place, as well as within the total context of space-time.[4] For it, the act includes all the inner determinations of the person as well as all its effects in space-time. And it is this relation of the whole act to the whole space-time that constitutes the religious dimension. Everything then is subject matter for the history of religions. The cultic and dogmatic have too long monopolized without challenge the definition of the religious; and the addition of the scriptural, of the theory of origin and destiny of man and cosmos, of the moral and of the aesthetic, and finally, of "the sacred" or "the holy" is certainly not enough. Every human act is religious in that it involves the inner person, the member of society, and the whole cosmos all at once, and all being, whether the so-called "sacred" or the so-called "profane," is the "religious." It was an impoverishment of the realm of the religious to limit it, as it were, to a unique act of man, to a unique aspect of his life, or to the sacred as opposed to the profane. The first two views are not compatible with our modern field theory of meaning, of value or of causation, where the particular is not a unique element, but a point in space-time at which converge and from which diverge an infinite number of elements in all directions.[5] The third denies half and more of the realities of the religious experience of mankind.

This restoration to the religious of its universal scope and relevance widens the horizons of the history of religions. Henceforth, it should include every branch of human knowledge and pursuit. For its purposes, mankind may still be divided into Christians, Jews, Buddhists, Hindus, Muslims, and other, but the whole history, culture and civilization of the Christians, Jews, the Buddhists, the Hindus, the Muslims, etc., should be its object.

B. The history of religions had its jurisdiction further curtailed in another direction. While, theoretically, it was supposed to be a history of all religions, it turned out to be in reality, a history of "Asiatic" and "primitive" religions on the one hand, and of the extinct religions of antiquity on the other. By far the overwhelming majority of the literature of the library of history of religions has been devoted to them. Judaism, Christianity and Islam always managed somehow to escape. This is not to plead that one group of materials is better, richer or more important than another. Primitive and ancient religions may very well hold for us many great lessons.[6] But they are far more impenetrable than the other group because of obstacles of language, of remoteness of time, of wide difference between their categories and ours. The truth that cannot be gainsaid here is that the comparativist has so far found the remoteness of primitive and ancient religions far more reassuring than the explosive character of the living world religions. Hence, he has been far bolder to collect the data of the former, to systematize, generalize about and judge them than the latter. He seems to have shied away, whether in awe or in panic, from handling the data of the living religions.

i. The Case of Islam

Islam had for a long time been engaged with the West in a hot colonialist war. The Muslim states bore the brunt of most European expansion in the 18th and 19th centuries. Islam was too "hot" to handle with a cool presence of mind and was allowed to become a subject for the missionaries to study in reconnoitering the field. With the development of the discipline, Islamics, a fair portion of this reconnaissance work passed on to secular hands. But these were more interested in helping the colonial office at home than in the discovery and establishment of truth. With the decline of the age of colonialism, an autonomous Islamics discipline came to life and, using the pioneer works of the previous generations of Islamists and the popularized mastery of the Islamic languages, Western knowledge of Islam developed very rapidly. All these considerations discouraged the serious student of comparative religion from studying Islam. While in the earlier stages the Western comparativist was a missionary, and as such disqualified from the study of the Islamic religio-culture, in the later stage (*viz.*, the stage of the secular Islamics discipline), he has been totally eclipsed by the Goldzihers, Schachts, Gibbs, Arberrys and men of like stature. So little is the Western historian of religions nowadays equipped in Islamics that that discipline, to which he has hardly contributed anything, does not seem to need him. Even today, no historian of religions proper has had anything to say that would catch the attention of the men of knowledge in the Islamics field. At the root of this shortcoming stands the fact that Islam was never regarded as an integral part of the subject matter of history of religions.

ii. The Case of Judaism

While the persistent witness of Judaism against Christ historically aroused fierce hatred and anti-Semitism, its close parental relation to Christianity accounted not only for the warmest admiration, but for Christianity's self-identification with the Hebrews of antiquity. As a result, the Christian mind was always confused regarding the phenomenon of Judaism as a whole. It sought clarity by dividing that phenomenon into two halves, "Before Christ" and "After Christ." Intellectually, and hence doctrinally, the latter half was a constant source of embarrassment and the ready solution that presented itself was to obliterate it, if not from the world, then from one's own mind. The former half became the object of Old Testament criticism; but this was never regarded as a branch of the comparative study of religion; that is to say, it was never treated independently of the categories of Christianity. Even where, as in Sigmund Mowinckel's *The Psalms in Israel's Worship* (R. A. P. Thomas, tr., Blackwell, Oxford, 1962), the whole purport of the study is, rather than "*Gattungsgeschichte*," the discovery of the *Sitz-im-Leben* in which the psalms – "the *fons et origo* of Christian hymnody"[7] – developed and crystallized as the only way to the understanding of what they could have meant to the Hebrew standing in the *sodh* of the temple, listening to or reciting them, the study is shot-through with Christian meanings and categories which were obviously introduced in order to show the ripeness of Hebrew consciousness to receive the Incarnation, its certain though hazy anticipation of the Christian dispensation, of "He that Cometh" which is the title of another work by that author.[8] Except where it was pursued as a Semitics discipline, Old Testament study was never an autonomous science, but remained to this day the handmaid of Christian theology. Where Old Testament studies developed as Semitic disciplines, they did achieve such autonomy; but they equally removed themselves from theology, history of religions and indeed the "Divinity Halls" of the universities in every case. Where the study remained within the "Divinity Halls," its highest objective, its *raison d'être*, never went beyond the confirmation of Christian dogma. The Christianist[9] strategy of thought could ill afford to put the Old Testament under the light of the comparative discipline. Hebrew scripture is, in this view, equally Christian scripture; Hebrew history, Christian history; and Hebrew theology, Christian theology. Hence, Old Testament criticism was confined to showing how Hebrew scripture is a scripture which, as the saying goes, was written "from faith to faith" – that is to say, written by people who believed in the divine scheme as Christianism understands it, for people who equally believe therein. Actually, another book, *i.e.*, a whole complexus of Christianist ideas, was pasted onto Hebrew scripture and Old Testament criticism was assigned the duty of keeping the paste moist and sticky. To this author's knowledge, no Christian theologian yet has dared to call Old Testament criticism by the only name it really deserves, namely, a part of the history of religions; and no historian of religions has yet attempted to rehabilitate the data of Old Testament criticism as integral to a reconstructed history of Hebrew and Jewish religion, rather than a *Heilsgeschichte*, or a history of the Father's manipulation of history as a prelude to the Incarnation.

iii. The Case of Christianity

Lastly, Christianity managed to escape from the history of religions because the greatest number of historians or comparativists held her above all the religions; indeed, as the standard bearer and judge of them. The limitation of the religious to the unique and personal act of faith confirmed this standard-bearing character of Christianity as the only one which fully realizes the meaning advocated.

History of religions is certainly fortunate in having at its disposal a very great amount of information collected over a whole century with great patience and labour. The great explorers and compilers of primitive religions have left an impressive legacy. The orientalists, Islamicists and students of Asiatic religions, the Old Testament critics, the Semiticists who developed out of Old Testament criticism autonomous Semitic and Ancient Near East disciplines, and the historians of the Christian Church, of Christian doctrine and of Christian civilization – all have contributed to present to history of religions its future subject matter. Undoubtedly, this subject matter is the greatest mass of human knowledge ever assembled. It would seem as if the work of history of religions we called reportage is all done and complete; but the truth is that a great deal more is required. Surely, sufficient knowledge has been accumulated to enable the history of religions to make a start in the second stage of systematization. But the future systematization of this knowledge needs a continuous activity of data-collection, the more fastidious and scrupulous the more exacting the work of systematization becomes. One systematization cannot refute and replace another unless it can marshall new data for its support or reveal new relations of old data which the first systematization had omitted. Invariably, this requires a mastery of the language or languages involved and a complete familiarity with the whole range of materials. The job which we called collection of data is really interminable.

2. *Construction of Meaning-Wholes or the Systematization of Data*
This great mass of data must be systematized; *i.e.*, ordered in three different operations:

Firstly, it should be classified in a way which answers the organizational needs of a modern enquiry. Under each heading the relevant data should be so analyzed and related to one another as to reveal the nexus of ideas of which they are the embodiment. The organization of the material must enable the modern researcher to put under the lucid light of consciousness, quickly and certainly, the whole field of ideas and all the particular items therein which, in any religion or aspect of a religion, constitute a single network or system of meanings. It should be topical as well as historical, and should endeavour to lay, at the disposal of the understanding, a comprehensive picture of all the facts pertinent to all topics, periods or groups within the religio-culture under examination. In turn, these complexi of data should be analyzed and related among themselves so as to disclose the essence of the religio-cuture as a whole.

Secondly, the relations of each datum with the whole complexus of history to which it belongs should be shown and established for thought. Its origin must be discovered, and its growth and development, its crystallization, and where necessary, its decay, misunderstanding and final repudiation must be accurately traced. Developments of ideas, institutions, of evaluations and discoveries, of human attitudes and deeds have to be projected against the background of historical facts. For they did not develop in the abstract but in a given milieu, and a need for precisely that development must have been felt. The datum in question must have been meant either to serve or to combat that development. Equally, every one of these developments must have had a whole range of effects which must be brought within the field of vision to be systematized if the understanding of the given data, the given movement, or the given system of ideas is to be complete.[10]

C. Thirdly, the religious data thus classified and systematized ought to be distilled for their meanings, and these meanings should be elucidated and systematized in turn. That is to say, they should be related as meanings, and not as facts as in the first two steps of systematization, to the historical complexus so that the civilization as such becomes both a structured whole of meanings and a whole with a meaning. Every religious datum, whether it is an expression of an idea, an attitude or feeling-state, a personal or social act, whether its object is the subject, society or the cosmos, whether it is a conceptual, discursive statement of the religious idea or act, or it is the religious idea or act itself, refers to something which is the content expressed, the meaning intuited or felt, the purpose realized or violated, or the object of inaction if no action whatever has taken place other than inaction. This something is a value. It is the meaning to which the religious datum is the human response, noetic, attitudinal or actional. As the human response could not become intelligible without its relation to the complexi of history, it cannot be meaningful without its relation to value. The former is a planar relation; the latter is a relation in depth. Unless the plane of historical relations is seen against the background of and is related to values in a depth relation, the religious datum may never be grasped for what it really is.[11]

In the discernment, analysis, and establishment of this depth relation – the relation of 'categorial existent' to 'axiological being' or value – history of religions meets serious perils and grave pitfalls. And it is true that a great number of comparative accounts of religions have failed in this requirement of constructing meaning-wholes out of the given religious data. But this failure is the failure of the investigator's own effort. It is not an argument against the history of religions or its methodology, but against the investigator and his research. Against the pitfalls of *eisagesis*, of reading into a religious datum something that is not there, or perceiving therein no value, or a value other than that which the adherent himself perceives, there is, in most cases, the religious wisdom of the adherents themselves. If a reconstruction meets the requisites of scholarship while at the same time the adherents of the religion in question find it meaningful and accept it as saying something to them about their own faith, surely, it has passed all that can be reasonably required of the comparativist. This was essentially the insight of W. C. Smith.[12] Certainly, the application of the principle presents a number of serious practical difficulties: The consent of which adherents of the faith may be taken as proof, and how may such consent be expressed? Moreover, it must be at least theoretically possible that the adherents of a religion may have gone so far in interpreting their religion that they have missed its primeval essence, that they do not find it any longer meaningful. This is of course tantamount to their acquiring a new religion, despite the fact that the new may still be called by the name of the old; and Smith's criterion cannot therefore be taken as a test of validity in the strict sense. Nonetheless, if we take it as a pedagogic principle, and ask the historian of religions to check his work, as it progresses, against the perspective of the adherents of the religion under investigation, we would have a check and balance technic to safeguard the work against aberration.

A stricter criterion of validity than an enlightened and scholarly application of Smith's pedagogic principle cannot be reasonably demanded. The adherent's naive argument, "Either you study my religion and therefore take into consideration what *I* think, *I* cognize, *I* intuit and *I* feel, or you study somebody else's," cannot be refuted. And as long as the reportage is a reportage on *him*, and the construction of meaning-whole is a systematization of meanings which *he* apprehends and relates in *his* own peculiar way, there is no escape from the recognition that the adherent's considered and scholarly judgment is final. If the historian of religion persists in his dissatisfaction, the only alternative open to him is to start a new investigation, a new reportage and a new systematization which he should distinguish from the first enquiry as he would two different religio-cultures.

The principle governing the work of systematization is therefore that the categories under which the systematizing works should proceed must be innate to the pertinent religio-culture investigated, not imposed thereon from the outside. The divisions constituting the various religio-cultures must not be interchanged, the data of each must be classified, analyzed and systematized not under categories alien to that religio-culture, but under categories derived from it. Those Christian investigations of non-Christian religions which systematize their materials under such categories as man's predicament; under ritual, law or sacrifice as atonement or salvation, etc., and speak of purity as morality, of the contrast of destiny to history, of redemption as the end and purpose of religion, betray an obvious governance by Christian principles which vitiates them. The suspicion that the investigation in question was carried out in order to show the deficiency of the non-Christian religion in the same areas where Christianity is claimed to be superior, can never be removed.[13] It is particularly here that history of religions shows its purely scientific character. Within the one religion, the task of organizing the data into a systematic whole, of relating doctrinal, cultic, institutional, moral and artistic facts to the history of the civilization concerned as a whole, is a purely scientific affair, despite the fact that the materials with which the historian of religions works are unlike those of the natural or social scientist. The scientific character of an enquiry is not a function of the materials, but of what is done with them.[14] The materials may be chemical facts or religious meanings. An enquiry into either is scientific if it starts from what is historically given and seeks to uncover the relations that govern the existence and actuality of these facts. It is immaterial that in one case the fact are laboratory materials in test tubes and in the other, ideas and facts recorded in books in a library or lived by a living community of men.[15] Certainly the "whats" in the two cases are different; but the presuppositions of methodology are the same. Just as the economist, the sociologist, the psychologist, the anthropologist apply the term "social science" to their scientific treatment of data other than those which can go into a test tube, we shall invent the term "humanitic science" to describe the history of religions' scientific treatment of materials other than those of the natural and social sciences. It is granted that religious as well as moral and aesthetic meanings are always instantiated in some overt social or personal behaviour and that, except through abstraction, they are really inseparable from their instances.

3. *Judgement or Evaluation of Meaning-wholes*

A. The Necessity of Judgement

However scientific and reliable these two operations may be, a history of religions which has accumulated as many scientific and reliable articulations and systematizations as there are religions is a mere boodle bag in which religio-cultural wholes have just been put one beside the other in eternal and cold juxtaposition. The first two steps of history of religions, therefore, justify the specialized disciplines of Islamic, Christian, Jewish, Hindu, Buddhist studies, and so forth; but not the history of religions as an autonomous discipline. For this, a third branch of study is necessary, *viz.*, judgement or evaluation. Out of the meaning-wholes constructed by the first two branches of history of religions, one meaning-whole should he arrived at, which would belong to man as such. Like the second, this third operation is also a systematization, not so much of particular data as of meaning-wholes. Its task is that of relating the given meaning-wholes to the universal, the human, and the divine as such. For this, meta-religion, or principles belonging to such order of generality as would serve as bases of comparison and evaluation of the meaning-wholes, is necessary. Such relating does involve a judgement of the individual meaning-wholes, an evaluation of their large claims. That this is itself a very large claim is not denied. Indeed, it sounds quite presumptuous to want to judge the religio-cultures of mankind. But the point is that the significance of the whole discipline of history of religions will stand or fall with the establishment or repudiation of this third branch.

i. First, we have seen that the first two branches can succeed in putting in front of us a series of internally coherent wholes of meanings, the constituents of each of which are related to one another as well as to their respective categorial existents manifest in the history, life and culture of that religion as well as to their respective axiological grounds. If the first two operations have been successful, and the religion in question is neither the Advaita School of Sankara or the Deuta School of Ramanuja Hinduism where all opinions, perspectives and judgements have absolutely the same truth-value, every meaning-whole will contain within it the claim not only that it is true, but that it is *the* truth. This claim is in a sense essential to religion. For the religious assertion is not merely one among a multitude of propositions, but necessarily unique and exclusive. It is of its nature to be imperative in addition to being propositive, and no command can issue therefrom if it did not mean to assert that its content is better or truer than the alternative content of another assertion if not the only true and good content *überhaupt*. Imperativeness is always a preference of something to something else; and this always implies that what is commanded in any instance is the best thing commandable in that instance. Where alternative commandments are of identical value, none may be said to be, by itself, commandable. Religious exclusiveness, when it is asserted not on the level of accidentals but on that of the essentials of a religion, can be dispensed with only at the cost of axiological relativism. For me to understand Christianity, for example, according to its own standards, and Christian thought as an autonomous expression of Christian experience is all well and good. But, if I ever omit from this understanding the claim that Christianity is a valid religion for all men, that the Christian faith is not only a true expression of what God may have done for some people but of what He has done or ever will do for the redemption of all men, of man as such, I am certain I would miss the essence and core. The same is of course true of all religions unless the religion is itself a sacralization of relativism, in which case it may not contend our assertion of exclusiveness without contradicting itself. What we then have in the boodle bag of the historian of religions is not a series of meaning-wholes, *simpliciter*, but a juxtaposition of several meaning-wholes each of which claims to be the only autonomous expression of the truth. These wholes do not only vary in detail, nor do they merely vary in the important issues. They diametrically contradict one another in most of the principles which constitute the framework and structure of their house of ideas. How then can the historian of religions, who is above all an academician, stop after the presentation of these wholes? As academician, the historian of religions is above all concerned with the truth. But to present the meaning-wholes of the religions and acquiesce to their pluralism is nothing short of cynicism. There is no alternative to this cynicism except in judging and evaluating the claimant meaning-wholes. The historian of religions must therefore do much more than steps 1 and 2.[16]

ii. Second, "knowledge" in history of religions does not consist merely of the apprehension of data. In science, a datum is gnoseologically valuable by itself, inasmuch as the natural fact held in conciousness is itself the end of the scientific investigation. In history of religions a datum has little history-of-religions-significance unless it is related to the feeling, propensity, aspiration or value-apprehension of which it is the expression, the affirmation or negation, the satisfaction or denial, the approbation or condemnation, the exaltation or denigration and so forth. But feelings, propensities, aspirations are human, not only Christian or Muslim, and value-apprehension is apprehension of a real value in experience. It is not therefore enough to know that for a certain religion, such and such are held to be facts. Movement from the Christianness or Muslimness of a factum to its humanness or universal reality is indispensable. Likewise, no meaning-whole is complete unless its insights, claims, *desiderata* and *damnata* are related to their human and therefore real roots, and thence to the real values and disvalues they seek to make real or to eliminate. Knowledge itself demands this relating to man as such, to existential and axiological reality. But to relate the data and meaning wholes in this manner is certainly to judge them. Mutually-contradictory as they are, to relate the data of religions or their meaning-wholes to the same reality, whether human or valuational, is really to present an incomplete picture with which the human understanding can do nothing. Indeed, such relating of them cannot be maintained in consciousness without coercion. But data which cannot be treated except coercively, *i.e.*, cannot be related to the universal and the real without dislodging or being dislodged by other data, cannot be simply true. Either the dislodging or the dislodged data are wrong, or their place in the meaning-whole has been wrongly assigned. The consequence, therefore, is that either the construction of the meaning-whole has been faulty or the meaning-whole as a whole has laid a false claim to the truth.

B. The Desirability of Judgement

Since the data which the historian of religions collects are universally related to meanings or values, they are, in contradistinction from the dead facts of natural science, life-facts. In order to perceive them as life-facts, an *époché* is necessary in which, as the phenomenologists have argued, the investigator would put his own presuppositions, religion and perspective in bracket while he beholds the given religious datum. This is necessary but insufficient. That the life-fact is endowed with energizing and stirring power implies for epistemology that to apprehend it is to apprehend its moving power in experience. Hence, life-fact cognition is life-fact determination, and to perceive a religious meaning is to suffer determination by that meaning. The historian of religions must therefore be capable of moving freely from one context to another while enabling his ethos to be determined by the data beheld alone. Only thus can he construct the historically given data into self-coherent meaning-wholes, which is his objective as historian of religions. But what does this peregrination mean for him as a human being, as a searcher for wisdom? And consequently, what does it mean for him to present to his fellowmen these mutually-repulsive, severally appealing and determining meaning-wholes?

It may be argued that the historian of religions should do no more than present these meaning-wholes from the highest level of detachment possible. Ivory-tower detachment is not only impressive but necessary when the subject matter investigated and presented to man belongs to the realm of nature which we called "dead facts." To apply it in the realm of life-facts, where to cognize is to be determined in discursive thought as well as in feeling and action is to expose men to their energizing power and moving appeal. Now, if the historian of religions takes no more than steps 1 and 2, he is exposing man to galaxies of meaning-wholes which pull him apart in different directions. There can be no doubt that every human being must reach his own personal decision regarding what is finally-meaningful, that the historian of religions is an academician who must remain absolutely aloof from all attempts to influence man's decision-making. But has he, by presenting to man merely the meaning-wholes in cold juxtaposition, *i.e.*, without relating them to the necessarily-universal, the necessary-real, the human, presented him with the whole truth? In this age of ours, when the world community has become conscious of a universal, human identity and is repeatedly calling for a discipline that will think out its spiritual problems as a human world community, has the ivory tower historian of religions, whose training has equipped him best for the job, the right to shy away? Does his shying away cast no doubt on his whole enterprise? By willing to preserve the religions of man frozen as they are, this ivory-tower scholarship detaches itself from the world of man and life that is constantly being made and remade and degenerates into superficiality.

These three considerations – the first two being theoretical, affecting knowledge of religions, and the third practical, questioning the wisdom of avoiding judgement – lead us to think that judgement is both necessary and desirable. There is hence no escape for history of religions from developing a system of principles of meta-religion under which the judgement and evaluation of meaning-wholes may take place. Although there have been many Christian theologies of history of religions, there is, as yet, unfortunately, no critical meta-religion. This shortcoming points further to the unpreparedness of modern Christendom to meet the world-community which is rapidly coming into being.

It is not the purview of this paper to elaborate a system of meta-religion. But it would indeed be incomplete if, having striven to establish its necessity and desirability, we omit to discuss its possibility.

C. The Possibility of Judgement

Perhaps the most common genre of meta-religion is that which looks upon the differences among religions as belonging to the surface, and upon their common agreements as belonging to the essence. This view does not always have to assume the superficial form it usually takes in inter-religious conventions where the "lowest common denominator" agreements are emphasized at the cost of all the difference. It can be sophisticated, as when it claims that underlying all differences, there is a real substratum common to all which is easily discoverable upon closer analysis. But it is nonetheless false because it seeks that substratum on the level of the figurizations and conceptualizations of the different religions where no such unity can be found except through selection of the materials investigated or a coercive interpretation of them. The profound differences that separate the religions on the level of teachings here all disappear in order to clear the road for generalization. When hindrances are found to be obstinate, they are subjected to an interpretation capable of bearing the required meaning. Such is the case of the analysis of Friedrich Heiler, who goes to great lengths to prove that all religions teach the same God and the same ethic, and whose conclusions are not even true to the theory of empirical generalization, not to speak of meta-religion whose principles must be apodictically certain. For him, Yahweh, Ahura Mazdah, Allah, Buddha, Kali, and – presumably, though his enumeration carefully omits him! – Jesus, all are "imagery" in which the one and same "reality is constantly personified."[17] Moreover, "this reality of the Divine" is identified as "ultimate love which reveals itself to men and in men;"[18] and "the way of man to God is universally the way of sacrifice."[19] Obviously this is to see the non-Christian religions with hopelessly Christian eyes, to bend the historically-given so as to accord with a predetermined Christian order.

Despite the fact that this sort of "scholarship" may serve to instill among the rank and file a little sympathy for "the others" who, hitherto, have been regarded as "infidels," "natives," etc., it remains at bottom a gratuitous condescension. As methodology of the history of religions, it is utterly worthless.[20]

A far more profound and philosophical theory of history of religions has been briefly laid out in an article by Professor B. E. Meland.[21] It too regards the religions as fundamentally one, not on the level of doctrine or figurization, but on that of a deeper lying substratum which is true – and seeks to reach, reconcile or judge the pronouncements of the different religions on the figurization level by reference to that deeper reality which is common to all. It is in the latter aspect that the theory runs aground. Whereas the unphilosophical theories fail because they do not seek humanity on the deeper level where it really is but on the figurizational level where it certainly is not, the philosophical theory of Professor Meland runs short because it seeks that reality on the level which properly belongs to it but identifies it in such a way as to make any knowledge – and hence any methodological use – of it impossible. Let us see how this is so.

Professor Meland analyzes the nature of man as consisting of three elements: First, "the primordial ground of the individual person as actualized event," *i.e.*, the primordial substratum of reality in which he has his being, his createdness. This deep-lying substrate is ontological and hence it transcends all particularisms; but "in its actuality … (it) is concrete." It is "man's life in God." It is "universal;" hence, "all concretion is ultimately due" to it. All perspectives, judgements, formulations of or within a religion "partake of this concreteness" and are, hence, "relative to it" in the "decisive" sense "that in this time and place reality has spoken." It "defines the base of our humanity" and gives man the capacity to understand the humanity of another.[22] Second, "the individuated selfhood of each person;" and third, "the cultural history in which the drama of corporate existence is enacted."[23]

In contrast to the first element which is universal, the second and third are specific and particular, and belong to the level of history and culture. It is true that neither the universal nor the particular is found without the other; but whereas the particular is readily and directly available for knowledge, the universal is never reached except through the particular. Thus the particular, which is a concretization of the universal, is relative thereto in the ontic sense; for it owes to the universal its very being. This may be granted. As to the availability of the universal for knowledge, Professor Meland rules out all hope for the historian of religions ever to attain it outside his own culture and concretization[24] on the grounds that "the structure of faith [*i.e.*, the particular] is so deeply organic to the individuation of the person in any culture ... [or so] much of this is below the level of conscious awareness ...[25] [that man's] processes of thought cannot escape or transcend its conditioning, however disciplined they may be."[26]

This reduction of all human knowledge to relativity, to the particular cultural structure of the subject (which Professor Meland calls the "fiduciary framework," borrowing the expression of Michael Polanyi), stems from a mistaking of relationality for relativity. The aforementioned ontic relation between primordial reality and its concrete actualization in space-time, which is the one-directional dependence of the particular to the universal, is here interpreted as epistemological and is turned around so as to become the absolute dependence of the universal to the particular. For this twist, however, no reason is given; and its net purport is the resolution to recognize only the particular as given, thus closing the gate of any reliable knowledge of the universal. But knowledge of the universal, of primordial reality, must be possible if the particular culture or religion, the "fiduciary framework," is not to be final. Passage from the particular to the universal, that is to say, the search for a meta-religion with which the particular may be properly understood as well as evaluated, is possible because, to parody the words of Kant, although all history of religions begins with the historically given data of the religions, the concrete religious experience of men in history, the given of the particular religions, it is not necessary that it all arise therefrom. Professor Meland too is keen to save this possibility, though he is opposed to any facile dogmatique of the universal. With this in mind, he suggested the method of negotiation of meaning in personal inter-religious encounter, asserting that the impenetrable opaqueness of meaning which the alien religion presents to the investigator could be dissipated by the encounter between him and the adherent of that religion, provided both are aware of their fiduciary frameworks, as well as of the fact that they are, as living concretizations of primordial reality, anchored in that one and the same reality. In such an encounter, Professor Meland holds, it would not be their particularistic dogmatique that carries the religious meaning sought, but the persons' saying such words as they do.[27]

One may ask, however, what does the adherent affirming and denying what he does affirm and deny, mean besides what is affirmed and denied which belongs to the level of the fiduciary framework? That the statement, 'Pete Smith, the American Christian, affirms that all men are sinful,' means more than the affirmation 'all men are sinful' is obvious. But what is not obvious is the meaning or relevance of the addition. Again, that the addition has a new meaning and relevance for the sociologist, the social psychologist, the demographist, the historians of all varieties (politics, economics, Christianity, civilization, etc.) studying American society, is obvious. But in all these cases, there is no implication that the fiduciary framework is going to be transcended, not to say that primordial reality, or the universal, is going to be reached. For encounter to serve the purpose Professor Meland has assigned to it, the new addition should have a meaning and a relevance to history of religions, that is to say, to the interest transcending the particular religions of the adherents, under which the latter could be illuminated, understood, evaluated and judged. But what is that meaning and relevance which must be other than what the psychologist, economist, historian and other social scientists are interested in? Professor Meland gave us no indication of it. How then can the desired "negotiation of meaning" be possible? How may that of which the religious figurization or fiduciary framework is the figurization be critically established for knowledge? Indeed, Professor Meland had already laid down that primordial reality is utterly unknowable. In this case, what reliance could be placed on any person's claim that in affirming and denying what he does, he is expressing "primordial reality"? How can the encounterer differentiate between the person communicating a particularized "primordial reality" and one communicating a particularized hallucination? Does any fiduciary framework express, take account of and constitute a concretization of "primordial reality" as well as any other? Are men absolutely free to develop any fiduciary framework they wish? Has not all human wisdom attained anything final at all concerning that primordial reality besides its *Dasein?* If these questions yield only negative results, then negotiated meaning is impossible and encounter is futile. If, on the other hand, the yield is positive, then certainly meta-religion is possible, and the historian of religions should apply himself to the task of elaborating it. In doing so, the historian of religions may not take the stand of skepticism. For to assert God and not to allow Him to be differentiated from a hallucination is idle, as it is for a Muslim to assert the unity of God and not that of truth, or for any rational being to assert reality and then to declare it many or utterly unknowable. To assert with Professors Polanyi and Meland that all we can ever have is a Muslimized or Christianized, Germanized or Russified version of the truth is skepticism – the denial of truth itself, including that of the skeptic's thesis, *à la* Epimenides.

The rock-bottom axiom of this relativism in religious knowledge is the principle that "the roots of man are in the region; or, more precisely, in that matrix of concrete experience, however much he may succeed in venturing beyond these psychic barriers through various efforts at shared experience."[28] Firstly, this is not self-evident. The contrary, namely, that the root of man is in the human universal rationality in which he partakes by nature, is quite conceivable. Nor can it be made to accord, secondly, with the wisdom of Biblical "J" which expressed men's universal brotherhood in their common descendence from Adam, and attributed their cultural peculiarities to environment.[29] Thirdly, it stems from an unfortunate fixation in the Western mind that whatever is, is first of all either French or German or English or Christian or Jewish, and is human, universal, real only in second place. This fixation is so chronic that the Western mind not only cannot see reality except as geographically, nationally, culturally or sectarianly determined, but goes on to assume that God created it so. "...Each [concrete occasion of reality] in its own circumstances, bodies forth its distinctive disclosure as an event of actuality, prehending the creative act of God with its own degree of relevance."[30] Evidently, that is the end of the road. It is relativism claiming for itself divine sanction.

And yet, if we can purge Professor Meland's theory of this relativist trait, we have left a genuine insight into the problem and a break-through to its solution. Certainly, what unites men of different fiduciary frameworks is, as Professor Meland says, their standing as actualizations of primordial reality, their createdness by one and the same Creator. Religiously speaking, the Creator has not only built in man His own image, *i.e.*, a capacity to transcend his creatureliness and recognize the Creator who is his source, but has taken several measures to bring to man a knowledge of Himself. Man therefore knows God, the primordial reality, if not naturally, then by means of revelation. On the other hand, *i.e.*, metaphysically speaking, the level of being at which man stands is differentiated from the lower levels of things, plants and animals, not only by that instrument of the will to live called the understanding, but by spirit, which enables man to cognize and evaluate his standing in Being's multilevelled structure. This is none other than Being's attainment of consciousness of itself. In man, Being judges itself. That it *has* often misjudged itself is the proof that it *can* judge itself, and consequently that it must, can and in fact does know itself. For it is as inconceivable that Being would enable the emergence of a creature that is a judge of Being without endowing it with the faculty to know the object of judgement, which is itself, as it is to find a being on any level that is not accompanied by the development of such cognitive faculties as enable the higher concretization of Being to fulfill that which distinguishes it from the lower and hence constitutes its *raison d'être*. That is what I gather from Professor Meland's profound insight; and it is a precious harvest indeed.

II
THE SIGNIFICANCE OF HISTORY OF RELIGIONS FOR CHRISTIAN EDUCATION

Pursued in its three branches, history of religions is the sovereign queen of the humanities. For, in a sense, all the humanities disciplines including the comparative ones are her front-line soldiers whose duties are the collection of data, their analysis, systematization and reconstruction into meaning-wholes. The subject matter of these disciplines is men's ideas and actions in all fields of human endeavour; and all these are, as we have seen, constituents in the religio-cultural wholes which history of religions proper studies as wholes, compares and relates to man and divinity in her attempt to reach the truth of both. The queen's concern is for every battlefield and hence for every individual soldier. But her real care is the headquarters kind of work which tells how and where the ship of humanity is going. History of religions, then, is not a course of study; it is not a department in a divinity school. It is, rather, by itself a college of liberal arts, each department of which is organically related to the center whose job is to make sense out of the infinite diversity of the religio-cultural experience, and thus contribute to the reconstruction of man's knowledge of himself, to his rehabilitation in an apparently alien cosmos, to his realization of value. Inasmuch therefore as history of religions is a collection and systematization of facts about human acts, life and relations, it is a college. Inasmuch as history of religions is an evaluation or judgement of meaning-wholes with the aid of a body of critical meta-religious principles, it is the queen of the humanities.

The fact is, however, that on any university or college campus these disciplines operate on their own in an autonomous manner without recognizing their organic relation to history of religions. This is not undesirable. First, a measure of evaluation and judgement relative to the data under immediate examination is necessary for collection and systematization work which is their duty, as we have seen earlier. Secondly, and in a deeper sense, their attempts at evaluation are desirable inasmuch as intellectual curiosity, or the will to know, is dependent upon the recognition of the unity of truth; *i.e.*, upon the realization that the discovery of truth is a discovery of a reality which is not divisible into unrelated segments but constitutes a unique and integral whole. Such realization is always a requisite for venturing into the unknown fields of reality. Thirdly, their evaluations and judgements are of inestimable value to the historian of religions, even though they may be biased or erroneous. They serve as a check and balance to the historian of religions whenever he is inclined to set the facts aside in favour of abstract constructionism. Such evaluation and judgement as the specialist data-reporter and systematizer are likely to make will at least be truer to the facts in question; and this is a need which history of religions can never overemphasize and no historian of religions can oversatisfy. Fourthly, history of religions herself should keep aware of these developments and be ready to evaluate the discoveries attained by these disciplines. Indeed, the task of evaluation is a necessary one and will be made by the discipline in question or by another at any rate. And the real issue is that of the need for and desirability of evaluation on the level of history of religions, that is to say, on the highest, the most comprehensive and critical level of all.

This is the place of history of religions in the university. What is its place in a school of divinity?

We have said earlier that the final purpose of history of religions is the putting under the light of consciousness the progress or movement of the ship of humanity towards truth, goodness and beauty. For this purpose, it works on its materials as it finds them historically fallen into the several religio-cultures of man, first by analyzing and systematizing them into autonomous meaning-wholes and then by evaluating their respective contribution to the progress of the ship of humanity towards those ideals. Obviously, Christianity is only one of the religio-cultures of humanity. Its history, with all that it contains, is the history of one of the religio-cultures of man, and, therefore, does not stand on the same level of generality as the history of religions. Nor can it in any way determine the work of the history of religions. The Christian may certainly hope that at the end of the road, Christianity's claims for embodying all truth, goodness and beauty will be confirmed; but he will have to allow it to stand in line with the other religio-cultures of man, in willful submission to the authority of judgement, that such a final vindication of his claim may be arrived at in a critical manner acceptable to all. A history of religions that is dominated or in any way influenced by Christianity, a history of religions which surreptitiously or openly seeks to vindicate Christian doctrine may be a handmaid of Christian theology, but not history of religions at all. This is so regardless of whether the materials studied are those of an extinct antiquarian religion, of a primitive religion with a handful of isolated adherents, or of a living world religion. Intellectual honesty is here most crucial, and must be satisfied before our loyalty to our religious traditions – indeed even at the cost of this loyalty if such sacrifice is necessary. And unless historians of religions agree on the priority of truth to Christian, Muslim, Jewish, Hindu, and Buddhist claims to the truth, then history of religions is doomed. The rules of the academic game, of the business of discovering and arriving at the truth, would be violated; and like the skeptics of latter-day value theory, the historians of religions may only seek to influence, to convert or subvert, but never to convince anybody of the truth. Therefore, the role of history of religions in a faculty of divinity cannot be in the least different from her role in a faculty of Islamic or Hindu studies. What is that role?

The material which history of religion studies is the history of religion; and in a divinity school, of Christianity. The history of Christianity covers a very long span of time and many peoples, and everything is important. But the purpose of history of religions' study of the history of Christianity is to trace the development of ideas, to lay bare for the ready use of reason, the genesis, growth and decay of Christian ideas against the background of social as well as ideological realities in the midst of which the ideational movement had taken place. The divine providential element cannot enter in this tracing as a factor, as a principle of explanation. This is not because history of religions is an atheistic science which does not believe in the presence of such element. On the contrary, the discovery of this element and its establishment for reason is the final purpose of the discipline as a whole. Rather, it is because divine providence never operates in the abstract, but always implies a plenum of real determinations. It is precisely the job of history of religions to discover this plenum, to analyze and expose its contents and relations. To admit the providential element here is *ipso facto* to put an end to the investigation. And since Christianity has not been an immutable and eternal pattern, frozen for all times and places, which the historian of religions can study once and for all, but a continuing development – that is to say, Christian history is not the development of a pattern, but the pattern itself is this development – the history of religions should find in the history of Christianity the richest field of ideational development.

To illustrate what I mean, let us take a closer look at the Old Testament. When the Reformation repudiated the religious authority of the Church, it vested that authority in the Scripture. When, later, the Christian mind rebelled against all authority except that of reason, sought enlightenment and observed a stricter moralism and a wider social liberalism, the Old Testament appeared inacceptable because of its running counter to these ideals. And with the Western Christian's discovery of "the world," the Old Testament's particularism, election, promise, remnant, and overdrawn political, social, and ideological history of the Hebrews lost its appeal and became something alien, whose acceptance depends upon fresh *Vergegenwärtigung*, or a making-meaningful-in-the-present, of its data. It was a great challenge which Christian scholars met by developing a critical science of the Old Testament. Out of this criticism a number of Semitic disciplines developed which added great contributions to human knowledge. And yet, there is hardly a Christian book on the Old Testament which does not try all sorts of *Heilsgeschichte* and allegorical interpretation acrobatics to reestablish the Old Testament as holy scripture *in toto*, though not verbatim; *i.e.*, to read into it by means of all kinds of *eisageses* a confirmation of the articles of Christian dogma.

True, the Old Testament as a record of the history and ideologies which surrounded, preceded, gave birth to or furnished the space-time human circumstance of revelation, is necessary. But Christian scholars do not read the Old Testament in this fashion. For them, it is all one consistent puppet-drama, operated by God to the end that the Incarnation, Crucifixion and Resurrection – in short, Redemption as Church dogmatics knows it – may result. To this author's knowledge, no Christian scholar and no historian of religions has as yet applied the techniques as well as the dogmafree perspective of history of religions to the Old Testament *as a whole*. As a result, no Christian thinker fully appreciates the revolution in religio-culture which Jesus initiated, for Christian dogma binds him to the notion that the Church is a new Israel, new to be sure, but nonetheless an Israel. The sanctity of the new Israel is thus extended to the old; and this bars any condemnation of old Israel, thus making it impossible to treat the breakthrough of Jesus as a revolution. For, a revolution is always against something. That something may be the circumstance of revolution, but it can never be good and desirable unless the revolution is bad and undesirable, and never divinely instituted unless the whole of history is equally manipulated by the divine hand. Nor was the revolution of Jesus directed only against one or two features of Hebrew religio-culture. It called for nothing less than a total radical self-transformation. A study of the Old Testament that is true to the discipline of the history of religions should show the genesis and development of that against which the revolution came, as well as the genesis and development of the stream of ideas of which the revolution came as an apex, as a consummation and crystallization.[31] That the two streams are present in the later parts of the Old Testament is granted. But the sifting of the two streams has never been done. Dulled by the constant attribution of sanctity to the whole history of Israel, the Christian mind has so far been unable to put the facts of this history under the proper perspective, and hence to distinguish the two streams: The nationalist particularist stream incepted by David, classicized and frozen by Ezra and Nehemiah; and the monotheic universalist stream of the non-Judah and other tribes the Shechemites within Palestine, the Aramaean kingdoms bordering on Palestine to the South and East, and generally, of the Semitic peoples migrating from the Arabian Peninsula – a tradition classicized by the Prophets and brought to the apex of revolution by Jesus. It takes the dogma-free history of religions to undertake a yet higher kind of Old Testament criticism, namely, to sift the Old Testament materials into that which is Hebraic or Judah-ic – which can never be Christian in any sense – and that which is universal, monotheic, ethical and Christian.

To take another example: Without a doubt the tradition of ideas which became the orthodox doctrine of Christianity is at least as old as St. Paul and probably as old as the Disciples. Equally, there must be no doubt that there were other traditions of ideas which were not as fortunate as to become Orthodoxy's dogma, but which were equally as old. Indeed, some of these other traditions were even prior. Firstly, they were essentially continuations of the Semitic tradition, whereas Orthodox Christianity built her ideational edifice primarily as a Hellenic structure. Secondly, if the advocates of the Old Testament have any point at all, it is certainly this that the divine revelation of Jesus has come within the space-time circumstance of the Hebrews, *i.e.*, within the Semitic ideological context of the Old Testament, not within that of Homeric Hellas, or of the Hellenized Near East and Roman Empire. The truth, therefore, cannot be controverted that the Semitic character of Ebionite Christianity, of the Arian, Marcionite and Paulician traditions, for example, stands far beyond question as prior to the Hellenic tradition which became the Orthodox doctrine. Hence the latter must be a "change" or "transformation" of the former. The Orthodoxy has coloured all Christian histories, and the most scholarly treatises still look upon the history of Christianity from the standpoint of the Orthodox dogma. Whereas we grant to the Orthodox historians the liberty to reconstruct their Orthodox tradition according to the categories of that tradition, what is needed is a history of Christianity which will present the various Christian traditions as autonomous meaning-wholes and then relate them to the Orthodox tradition in a way revealing as well as explaining the differences. Only such a history would be truly instructive concerning the formative period of Christianity – the first seven centuries. Only it will be concerned to tell the whole story of this development against the historical background of the social and ideological realities of the Near East and Roman Empire. The Orthodox evaluation of these traditions is valuable for the light it sheds on itself, not on the traditions it condemns. It is unfortunate but challenging that no scholar has as yet used the source materials of the history of Christian ideas in the first seven centuries in order to bring to light the genesis and development of these diverse Christian traditions connecting them with the Semitic consciousness, the Hellenic consciousness or the mixed-up Semitico-Hellenic consciousness of the Near East (which all Christian historians confusedly call "Eastern Christianity," "Eastern Churches" and the like). That remains the task of the historian of religions in the field of Christian history. For it is he who, while rightly expected to read the Orthodox tradition under categories furnished by that tradition alone, is equally rightly expected to read the history of the other Christian traditions under their own categories, and then judge them all under the principles of meta-religion.

III
THE SIGNIFICANCE OF HISTORY OF RELIGIONS FOR THE CHRISTIAN-MUSLIM DIALOGUE

These two illustrations have not been picked up at random. Together, they constitute not only the common grounds between the three world religions of Judaism, Christianity and Islam, but equally the most important fields of contention between them. And of the three religions, Christianity and Islam are here perhaps the most involved. The work that awaits the historian of religions in these two areas will contribute decisively towards constructive dialogue between these religions in addition to re-establishing a very important segment of the religious history of the majority of mankind.

The Old Testament is not only Hebrew scripture (or the divine law revealed to Moses and the nationalist history of an extremely particularist people) nor only Christian scripture (or, according to the dominant *Heilsgeschichte* school, the inspired record of God's saving acts in history culminating in the Incarnation). It is also Islamic scripture, inasmuch as it is the partial record of the history of prophecy, and hence of divine revelation.[32] Indubitably, every one of these religions can point to something in the Old Testament substantiating its claim. But the whole truth cannot be on the side of any. Furthermore no religion is, by definition, equipped to transcend its own categories so as to establish the historical truth of the whole which, as a religion, it interprets in its own way in order to suit its own purpose. Only the historian of religions measures to the task who would relate the ideas of the Old Testament to the history of the Hebrews as ancient history has been able to reconstruct it, holding in *épochè* both the Christian and the Islamic understanding of Hebrew scripture. But we may not make total abstraction of the Hebrew understanding because the Old Testament is, after all, a Hebrew scripture written in Hebrew by the Hebrews and for the Hebrews. The contents however are not strictly speaking all Hebrew materials. The ideological overtones of the scripture, namely, those set in the books of Genesis and Exodus, are Hebrew versions of Semitic themes which belong to all Semites. Islam is a Semitic religion whose formative years were spent in Arabia, the cradle of all things Semitic. It is natural that the Islamic version of these themes is another version of ideas which are much older than "J." The Islamic claim may not therefore be brushed aside as external to the matter in question. For just as Christianity is "a new Israel," Islam is "an other Israel" legitimately giving a version of Semitic origins which are as much, if not more, its own as that of the Hebrews.

Secondly, the examination by history of religions of the formative centuries of Christianity is equally involving for Islam. Islam is not a foreigner here. Islam is Christianity inasmuch as it is a moment in the developing Semitic consciousness of which the Hebrew, Judaic and Christian religions were other moments. That is why Islam rejected neither the Hebrew Prophets nor Jesus but, recognizing the divine status of their missions, reacted to the assertions of Jews and Christians regarding them. Although the Prophet Muhammad and his first Muslim followers were personally neither Jews nor Christians, yet their ideas were in every respect internal to the Jewish and Christian traditions, affirming, denying and in some cases transcending what Jews and Christians have held to be or not to be the faith of Adam, of Abraham, of Noah, of Jacob, of Moses and of Jesus. The "Christianity" which Islam is, therefore, is an alternative to Orthodox Christianity; but it is as much Christianity as Orthodox Christianity is. Neither is Islam's Christianity an alternative posed *in abstracto*, as a discursive contradiction or variation, but *in concreto*, a historical alternative. Islam too did not come about except "in the fulness of time" but this fulness consisted in the attempt by Orthodox Christianity to wipe out the Christian alternatives to itself. In the first century of Islam, the greatest majority of its adherents had been Christians in disagreement with Orthodox Christianity concerning what is and what is not the revelation and religion of Jesus Christ. Islam is certainly a Christian revolution with as much connection to Jesus as Orthodox Christianity can claim. We should not be misled by the fact that the Islamic revolution within Christianity reached farther than what it had originally set out to accomplish. The fact is that Islam was no more new than the religion of Jesus was in respect to the religion of the Jews. The continuity of Jesus' prophetic thought with the spiritualizing and internalizing thought of Jeremiah and the pietism of Amos and Micah is recognized and confirmed by Islam. Jesus' ethic of intent is, in Islam, the *sine qua non* of morality. Jesus' notions of the unity of the Father, of His fatherhood to all men, and of his love-of-neighbour – in short, his ethical universalism, is not only honored by Islam but rediscovered as essence of that Semitic consciousness which chose to migrate from Ur as well as from Egypt.[33] On the other hand, the opposition of Jesus to Judaic particularism is universalized in Islam as the opposition of the universal brotherhood under the moral law to all particularisms except the Arabic Qur'an which is the expression of this opposition. Therefore, there can be no doubt that Semitic Christianity had itself developed into Islam, and that the latter's contention with Orthodox Christianity is only a backward look within the same stream from a point further down its course – in short, a domestic recoupment within the one and same Semitic consciousness itself.

Despite this domestic nature of the contention between Islam and Christianity, neither Christianity nor Islam is really capable of going over its categories in the examination of the historical facts involved. Only a complete suspension of the categories of both, such as history of religions is capable of, holds any promise. The historical truth involved must be discovered and established. If, when that is done, either Christianity or Islam continues to hold to its old versions and views, it would do so only dogmatically, not critically. And we may hope that under the impact of such reestablishment of the formative history of Semitic consciousness in its Judaic, Christian and Islamic moments, the road would be paved for some dogma-free spirits, loyal to that consciousness, to prepare the larger segment of mankind for meeting the challenge of the world-community. So too, such reestablishment of the history of Semitic consciousness makes possible a new reconstruction of Christian religious thought which does not suffer from dependence upon epistemology. From the days of Albert the Great, attempts at reconstruction have been made on the basis of the philosophy that is currently in vogue. That is why every systematic theology, or reconstruction, fell down with the fall of the epistemological theory on which it was based. That is why the current systematic theologies will also fall as soon as a new epistemology rises and establishes a reputation for itself. What is needed is a reconstruction "supra-philosophies," which does its work within the Orthodox doctrine without external aids, by reinvestigating its formative period. This doctrine, as the Orthodoxy itself holds, is largely the work of men, of Christians, of majority-resolutions or otherwise of synods and councils, whose "inspired" status ought to be once more investigated. A reconstruction that does not reopen the questions resolved at the Pre-Nicene Synods, at Nicaea (325), at Constantinople (381), at Ephesus (431), and at Chalcedon (451) will not answer the demands that have been made by Muslim converts from Christianity and are now beginning to be heard from the more recent Christian converts in Asia and Africa. It is not surprising that voices like that of the Rev. U. Ba Hmyin made itself heard at the last Assembly of the World Council of Churches at New Delhi calling for a reconstruction of Christian doctrine as radical as the Hellenic transvaluation was of Semitic Palestinian Christianity.[34] What is surprising is the fact that the World Council never responded to this formidable challenge.[35] The greater trouble, however, is not the impending doctrinal separation of Afro-Asian Christianity from Western Christianity, but the increasing impatience with or lethargy to this Western doctrine on the part of lay Western Christians. The soul of the modern Christian is unmoved by the doctrinaire assertions of *Heilsgeschichte*, of the fallenness of man, of the trinitarian conception of divinity, of vicarious suffering, of ontic Redemption, of the elected and exclusivist status of the Church. What is needed is a genuinely new rebirth. And it is a rebirth which must begin by saying a resolute "No!" to Irenaeus's claim that "... Those who wish to discern the truth ... [must do so in] the tradition and creed of the greatest, the most ancient church, the church known to all men, which was founded and set up at Rome by the two most glorious apostles, Peter and Paul. For with this church, because of its position of leadership and authority, must needs agree every church, that is, the faithful everywhere ..."[36] What the Christian participant in the Semitic stream of consciousness needs is to outgrow the unchristian fixation of Irenaeus which asserts: "There is now no need to seek among others the truth which we can easily obtain from the church [of Rome]. For the Apostles have lodged all that there is of the truth with her, as with a rich bank, holding back nothing ... All the rest are thieves and robbers ... The rest ... we must regard with suspicion, either as heretics and evil-minded; or as schismatics, puffed up and complacent; or again as hypocrites, acting thus for the sake of gain and vain glory."[37] For this, history of religions must teach the Christian anew, against the wisdom of Tertullian,[38] that Apostolic Succession – even if its historicity is granted – can be an argument only if the heirloom is biological or a thing that can be given and taken without suffering change; that since the "heirloom" is ideational, and in the absence of a Jesus-Qur'an frozen verbatim with the categories under which it can be understood as it must have been by its mouthpiece, the decisions of the Church of Rome stand on a par with the pronouncements of a Priscilla-Miximilla team, and those of Irenaeus on a par with those of a Cerinthus.

Notes

1. A lecture delivered to the faculty of the Divinity School of the University of Chicago, on April 30, 1964, in the course of the author's residence as guest-researcher at the said institution. Professor Bernard E. Meland, Professor of Constructive Theology, and Professor Charles H. Long, Professor of History of Religions, read critical responses. The response of the former appears at the end of this article. That of the latter, consisting largely of notes, appears in footnotes appended to the article where they are relevant.
2. Prof. Long's note: "Dr. Faruqi's portrayal of the history of the discipline of history of religions presupposes that the history of this discipline was carried out along lines which were quite rational. Such was not the case. The history of religions is a child of the enlightenment. This is to recognize that the history of religions had its beginnings in a period in which the western world was seeking some rational (as over against a religious) understanding of the history of man's religious life. The history of religions during the enlightenment was for the most part rationalistically and moralistically oriented. Prior to this time, the understanding of religion from a religious point of view yielded even less on the level of scientific understanding, for while the medieval theologians were able to see Islam, for example, as a religion and not as an instance of a truncation of reason, it was nevertheless relegated to the level of paganism since it did not meet the standards of the one true revelation. The rationalistic interpretation of history had the value of establishing a criterion other than revelation as the basis of religion. This meant that to a greater degree the data of the non-Christian religions could be taken a bit more seriously. This along with the universalism of the enlightenment and the reports from colonizers and missionaries established a broader if inadequate basis for the understanding of other religions and cultures, though in several instances the final revelation of God in Jesus Christ was transformed into the final apotheosis of reason in the enlightenment civilization of the western world."
3. Prof. Long's note: "The definition of religion as 'the Holy' or the sacred was

an attempt to save the religious life of mankind from a reduction to dimensions of life which were inadequate as interpretative schema for the data which had been unearthed. The development of methodologies in this direction was directed against not only the understanding of non-Western religion, but equally at the rationalistic and moralistic understanding of western religion. It is not therefore strange that among the leading historians of religion are to be found a Lutheran archbishop and a German theologian. Participation in the religious life itself sensitizes one to the availability of the religious reality for all men in all times and places. Rudolf Otto advised those who thought the religious experience impossible to lay aside their books, and Nathan Söderblom stated that he knew there was a living God, not because he was a Christian, but because all religions testified to this fact. To be sure, as Dr. Faruqi implies, the work of Otto and Söderblom restricted the meaning of religion, but only to save it and they were aware always of the relationship of the holy to the totality of man's life; witness for example, Otto's schematization which attempted to place all of the important dimensions of human life as originating in and deriving their sense of importance from the obligation of the holy in religious experience. This specificity of the holy was paralleled with a specificity of the historical – religious object – the recognition of the individual, ineffable and unique in history. This derationalizing or in some cases, irrationalizing of history grew out of their methodological approaches and constituted a critique of the rationalizing tendency of some of the prevailing philosophies of history – philosophies stemming from Kant and Hegel. In transforming the data of religion, historically defined, into rational notions, the rational notions prevailed as the criteria of supreme validity; the religious basis of evaluation, *i.e.*, revelation, was at most a provisional step towards a rational view. I submit that what Dr. Faruqi describes as the Christianizing and misunderstanding of Judaism and Islam derives from this tendency and not from the *main line* historians of religions. It should also be noted that the same rationalizing tendency operated in the case of primitive Hindus and Buddhists. The notions of the ineffability, irrationality, and irreducibility of the religious were designed to make a place for, or to hold open the criterion of validity which arises out of, the historical-religious data itself. The relationship or re-introduction to the validity of religion to all of life become the perennial problem of the discipline."

4. The sense in which it does so will become clear as we discuss the systematization and judgement functions of history of religions, *infra*, p. 43 ff; p. 50 ff.
5. Ushenko, Andrew Paul, *The Field Theory of Meaning*, U. of Michigan Press, Ann Arbor, 1958, p. III ff.
6. Consider, for a case in point, Professor Mircea Eliade, whose works (*Images et Symboles*, Gallimard, Paris, 1952; *Mythes, rêves et mystères*, Gallimard, Paris, 1957; *Patterns in Comparative Religion*, Sheed and Ward, London, 1958; *Birth and Rebirth*, Harper and Row, New York, 1958; *The Sacred and the Profane*, Harper and Row, New York, 1959; *Cosmos and History: The Myth of the Eternal Return*, Harper and Row, New York, 1959; etc.) constitute the worthiest attempt of the discipline to "*vergegenwärtigen*" the archaic religions. "We hold," Prof. Eliade writes in the foreword to his interpretive work, *Cosmos and History*, "that philosophical anthropology would have something to learn from the valorization that pre-Socratic man – in other words, traditional man – accorded to the universe. Better yet: that the cardinal problems of metaphysics could be renewed through a knowledge of archaic ontology." Regardless of whether or not the book substantiates it, the claim by itself has grave significance not only for the discipline of history of religions in whose name it is made, but for "the philosopher, and ... the cultivated man in general ... for our knowledge of man and for man's history itself."

   Another recent case in point is Charles H. Long's able argument for the claim that "as a religious norm, it [monotheism] has always been there – an enduring structure of the religious experience itself." ("The West African High God," *History of Religions*, Vol. III, No. 2, Winter, 1964, p. 342).
7. Mowinckel, *op. cit.*, Preface, p. xxii.
8. We should not mistake the advocates of *Religionsgeschichteschule* for historians of religions. Those who were not secularists were Old Testament theologians who, having faith in the dogma, interpreted the findings of Ancient Near Eastern history and accommodated them in what they called *Heilsgeschichte*. Herman Gunkel, perhaps the most famous name in that school, is a committed Old Testament theologian who asserts explicitly, in criticism of Frantz Delitzsch's famous lectures *Babel and Bible* (tr. by C. H. W. Johns, G. P. Putnam's Sons, New York, 1903) that "in the depth of this development [Israel's history] the eye of *faith* sees God, Who speaks to the

soul, and Who reveals Himself to him who seeks Him with a whole heart." It would be utterly misleading to call him a historian of religions or to identify his methodology as "history of religions." indeed, Gunkel is so committed to his theological ideas that, in the same "critique," (it reads more like a sermon) – he bursts into exclamations: "What sort of a religion is it (the religion of Israel)? *A true miracle of God's among the religions of the ancient orient!* ... He who looks upon this religion with believing eyes will confess with us: To this people God hath disclosed Himself! Here God was more closely and clearly known than anywhere else ... until the time of Jesus Christ, our Lord! This is the religion on which we depend, from which we have ever to learn, on whose foundation our whole civilization is built; we are Israelites in religion even as we are Greeks in art ... etc., etc." (*Israel and Babylon: A Reply to Delitzsch*, John Jos. McVey, Philadelphia, 1904, p. 48) Evidently we must be very careful in calling men "historians of religions," when "historian of Old Testament" or "historian of Christianity" would be far more appropriate.

9. "Christianism" is the movement which, though older than Nicaea (325 A.C.), emerged from that council as orthodox Christianity, upholding a specific dogma – the Nicene Creed – as exclusively definitive of the faith of Jesus.

10. This has been well pointed out by Joseph M. Kitagawa in the opening essay on "The History of Religions in America" in *The History of Religions: Essays in Methodology*, ed. Kitagawa, J. M. and Eliade, M., University of Chicago Press, Chicago, 1959, where he says: "... One must study the historical development of a religion, in itself and in interaction with the culture and society. One must try to understand the emotional make-up of the religious community and its reaction or relation to the outside world ... There must be added a religio-sociological analysis, in our sense of the term, the aim of which is to analyze the social background, to describe the structure and to ascertain the sociologically relevant implications of the religious movement and institutions." (p. 26).

11. To take an example from this author's forthcoming study of Christianity: 'The Fall' or 'Original Sin' is a datum of the Christian religion. We must first understand what it means discursively, by reading the definition and analyses of Hebraic and Jewish thinkers for the Old Testament precursors, and of Christian thinkers from the New Testament to P. Tillich. Having

grasped the doctrinal development of the idea, we then relate it to the historical development of Christendom, showing how, in every stage, the Fall developed in answer to certain sociological and doctrinal developments. Thus systematized into a developing stream of complexi of ideas, each member of which is a network of a number of closely-related facts, this complex religious datum is then related in depth to the values which at each stage of the development, the datum was meant to and actually did, serve to realize. This last relation is usually more evident in the general literature of the civilization than in the strictly doctrinal statements.

12. "No statement about a religion is valid unless it can be acknowledged by that religion's believers." (Smith, W. C., "Comparative Religion: Whither – and Why?," *The History of Religions: Essays in Methodology, cit. supra*, p. 42).

13. See Fazlur Rahman's and this author's reviews of Kenneth Cragg's *Call of the Minaret* and *Sandals at the Mosque*, in *Kairos*, 3-4, 1961, pp. 225-233.

14. Prof. Long's note: "I cannot deny that the discipline consists of reportage and collection of data, construction of meaning wholes and judgement and evaluation, but these areas of the discipline cannot be separated so neatly; each one implies the other. It is on this basis that I take exception to Dr. Faruqi's statement that, 'The scientific character of an enquiry is not a function of the materials, but of what is done with them.' I should rather emphasize the fact that the scale determines the phenomenon. It is the method which gives us our data and this method represents a complex relationship between the objectivity and the relatedness of the data to the interpreter. This is what lay behind the *Methodenstreit* in Germany in the last century. Are there real differences between the constitution of the data of the human sciences and the natural sciences? Does the scale really determine the data? While I am not satisfied with the bifurcation which represented a resolution of the problem, I appreciate the problem. I would rather restate the problem in a different way. 'Is it possible for us to understand the human mode of awareness which presents reality to us as a totality?' Some forms of process philosophy take this question quite seriously but within the history of religions the analyses of primitive and traditional religions tend to describe the human awareness in these terms. Again, the sacred or the holy becomes an appropriate way of dealing with this issue."

15. It was this consideration that misled Professor Kitagawa to assign to the

history of religions a position intermediate between descriptive and normative. (*Op. cit.*, p.19). He clearly saw the descriptive nature of the discipline when it studies the history of a religion, or when it appropriates the analyses of psychology, anthropology, sociology, philology, etc., and of scriptures, doctrines, cults and social groupings. But when he came to differentiate history of religions from the normative disciplines, he wrote: "While *Religionswissenschaft* has to be faithful to descriptive principles, its inquiry must nevertheless be directed to the meaning (*sic*) or religious phenomena." (Ibid., p.21). This concern with meanings is, in his view, sufficient to remove history of religions from the ranks of descriptive science. Evidently, he precludes the possibility of a descriptive treatment of normative content such as value-realist philosophy has been suggesting for a generation. (*cf*. the tradition of Max Scheler, Nikolai Hartmann, etc.)

16. Prof. Long's note: "This point of Dr. Faruqi is well taken. It has to do with the inter-relationship of meaning wholes. From a study of religions, we now ask, what is religion. I also concur in his criticism of Prof. W. C. Smith's criterion for valid interpretation. I must however question the presuppositions underlying the very constitution of the meaning-wholes. For the historian of religion, such meaning-wholes exist but not simply as geographically and culturally defined units. The historian of religions should not begin his study by setting aside a certain number of religions and taking them in order to study them one after another. He should rather begin with forms of the religious life and an exhaustive study of these forms already leads him out of simply geographically and culturally defined units. The very fact that he supposes that he can understand that which is other leads him to a wide range of religious data. The meaning wholes are for him already inter-related and thus the problem of their relationship is of a different kind. I am one of those historians of religions who does not like to hear the question put as the relationship of Christianity to the non-Christian religions. For me the issue is put more precisely when we ask the meaning of religious forms as valid understanding of man's nature and destiny. Any discussion of this issue leads us to empirical data, but it also implicates us in a discussion which enables us not only to talk about the resources of our peculiar traditions, but also the resources of a common humanity – a common humanity which all living religionists may claim."

17. "The History of Religions as a Preparation for the Cooperation of

Religions," *The History of Religions: Essays in Methodology*, p. 142.

18. Ibid., p. 143.
19. Ibid., pp. 143-144.
20. Other examples betraying the same shortcoming are Albert Schweitzer's *Christianity and the Religions of the World*, Allen and Unwin, London, 1923; Hendrik Kraemer, *Why Christianity of all Religions?*, Westminster Press, Philadelphia, 1962; Stephen Neill, *Christian Faith and Other Faiths: The Christian Dialogue with Other Religions*, Oxford University Press, 1961; A. C. Bouquet, *The Christian Faith and Non-Christian Religions*, James Nisbet and Co., London, 1958; Jacques-Albert Cuttat, *La Rencontre des Religions*, Aubier, Editions Montaigne, Paris, 1957; R. C. Zaehner, *The Convergent Spirit: Towards a Dialectics of Religion*, Routledge and Kegan Paul, London, 1963; etc.
21. "Theology and the Historian of Religion," *The Journal of Religion*, Vol. XLI, No. 4, October, 1961, pp. 263-276.
22. Ibid., p. 265.
23. Ibid., pp. 265-266.
24. Ibid., p. 272.
25. Ibid., p. 261.
26. Ibid., p. 275. Here Professor Meland finds himself in agreement with Michael Polanyi (*Personal Knowledge*, University of Chicago Press, 1958, p. 266) who identifies the particular for knowledge as "fiduciary framework" outside of which "no intelligence, however critical or original, can operate." (Meland, *op. cit.*, p. 271).
27. Ibid., pp. 274-275.
28. Ibid., p. 264.
29. Genesis, II: 1-9.
30. Meland, *op. cit.*, p. 265.
31. By distinguishing "the earthly Jesus" of history from "the heaven-exalted Christ" of dogma and "the Pre-existent Logos" of doctrine, Shirley Jackson Case had an edge on the problem (*Jesus: A New Biography*, The University of Chicago Press, Chicago 1927, pp. 2-5) which he lost in the presentation of the earthly Jesus. Discarding the evidence of the Gospels as projection onto the past of animosities and oppositions pertinent to the Church of the first and second centuries A.C., Case regarded Jesus' task as being merely one of "summon[ing] the Jewish people to a life in more perfect accord with

the will of their God" (Ibid., p. 264), of "deliver[ing] ...a message of warning designed to augment righteousness in Israel" (Ibid., p. 342). This task, anticipated and fulfilled by John "calling upon the people of Palestine to reconsecrate themselves to God in preparation for the Day of Judgment" (Ibid., p. 242), "had first aroused the interest of Jesus" at his baptism and was adopted by him incidentally on account of "a heightening of emotion [attending his experience of baptism] that impelled him to assume the responsibilities of a new life-work." (Ibid., p. 257). Indeed, Jesus did not even envisage any global mission at all; for "the range of his activities widened [only] when Jesus paid a visit to 'the borders of Tyre and Sidon,' which provided a setting for the story of his generous attitude toward the Syro-phoenician woman." (Ibid., p. 269) The task of Jesus is thus diluted into one of simple reform. It was not a revolution against the moral decadence, tribalism and vacuitous legalism of Judaism evidenced in both the Gospels and the Talmud because, for Case, there was no need for one "Jesus ... [having] more in common with them [Scribes and Pharisees] ... in his sympathies and aims ..." (Ibid., pp. 304-305), and "fundamentally, the difference between Jesus and the contemporary religious leaders of Judaism ... [being] one of personal and social experience ... [merely] a neglect of legal niceties ... [and his being a plebeian or] 'Amme ha-aretz' unhabituated to the more meticulous demands of the scribal system." (Ibid., p. 315) Where the Gospel evidence to the contrary is not due to the personal character of Jesus and his being untutored in the Law, Case regards it as "occasional instances of conflict due to personal pique." (Ibid., p. 316) Obviously all this theorizing is due to Case's commitment to that aspect of Christian dogma which asserts the holiness of the Jewish people, as well as of their religious principles and practices as given and recorded in the Old Testament – a holiness which precludes all significantly original changes, even if God Himself is the author, and Jesus the instrument of the change. Case's "Life of Jesus" is "a new biography" as far as the "heaven-exalted Christ and Pre-Existent Logos" are absent from it. But it is not historical and hence not properly-speaking a work of the history of religions.

32. Faruqi, I. R. al, "A Comparison of the Islamic and Christian Approaches to Hebrew Scripture," *The Journal of Bible and Religion*, Vol. XXXI, October, 1963, No. 4, pp. 283-293.

33. For a detailed analysis of the circumstances of these two migrations, see this

author's *On Arabism: Vol. I, 'Urubah and Religion*, Djambatan, Amsterdam, 1962, pp. 18-28.

34. "When Christian witnesses moved out of the world of Jewish thought and understanding into the wider world of Greek language, thought and life, it was one of the most profound changes and crises of the Church. Greek thought, forms, language and modes of apprehension were taken over, and have since become part of the very life of the Church. These have become such a part of Christian theology, that it is easy to see why some Asian people think that the Christian Gospel is intimately related to Western man. But now the Gospel has taken root in Asia. The question before us is: Is it possible to make the radical break from purely Western ways of thought, to do in Asia what first-century Christians did in the Greek world? It is possible to utilize structures, ways of thought and life which are Asian even as Greek expressions have been used? This is not a simple question. It is often asked, if this was not a corruption of the Christian message as expressed in its Hebrew forms. But some such use was both possible and necessary for the Church to go about its missionary task. Such an effort seems both possible and necessary today. And it might well prove to be the greatest challenge that the Church has faced since the transition from Jewish soil to Greek soil was made. If theology is to be ecumenical it must be able to utilize and confront systems and ways of thought and life other than those known as Western. No theology will deserve to be called ecumenical in the coming days which ignores Asian structures. It may use the term ecumenical, but it will really be parochial and Western only." (Assembly Documents, No. 1, November 19, 1961, New Delhi). It is noteworthy that this Christian Asian leader regards the Roman-Hellenic interpretation of Palestinian Christianity "a profound change" as well as "a corruption of the [original] Christian message."

35. As far as this author could gather, whether from the papers of the World Council of Churches Third Assembly at Delhi or from his interviews with a number of delegates to the Assembly, Rev. Hmyin's message passed "like water on the back of a duck." And in the report of the East Asian Section of the Theological Commissions to the Fourth World Conference on Faith and Order (Montreal, 1963) the formidable issue of Rev. Hmyin was neither discussed nor given statement in the findings. Indeed, the whole field of "Christian Thought and Theology" was merely listed as one of the "areas

calling for a greater effort towards indigenization," as well as put under the express condition that such indigenization would not involve "diminution of Catholic truth." A statement of this "catholic truth" (obviously written by the secretary of the East Asian Section, Rev. J. R. Fleming, a Western Christian, for his East Asian colleagues) was entered in the Findings of the Montreal, 1963 meeting, in which we read: "Christian worship is the glad response of the people of God to the gracious redemptive activity of God the Father, and Christ the Son, through the Holy Spirit. Christian Worship therefore is both Christological and Trinitarian. To say it is Christological means that the central act in Christian worship is the proclamation of the good news of God's redemption and re-creation of humanity in Christ ... This Christological worship is both individual and corporate, but the primary emphasis is on the corporate, since God's purpose in Christ is to create a new body of people, Christ's body. In Christian worship, therefore, man ... becomes a part of the new humanity in whom God's purposes in creation are being fulfilled. His life is defined now in relation to God in Christ, and in terms of *leitourgia* and *latreia* ... To say Christian worship is Trinitarian means that it is offered to God in the light of this revelation of himself as Father, Son and Holy Spirit. Because God is known in Christ, He is known as creator, for whose gracious purposes in creation men are now reclaimed and redeemed ..." etc. (*Faith and Order Findings*, Montreal, 1963, SCM Press, Ltd., London, 1963, Report of the Theological Commission, pp. 32, 39). Obviously this is a report of 1963 Western Christian thought which the Asian representatives have been "buffaloed" into countersigning. Or, if the voice of Rev. Hmyin is representative, however little, of Asian-African thought, the foregoing is a report of what the parent Western churches of 1963 had wished the Asian churches to regard as "Catholic truth."

36. Irenaeus, *Against Heresies*, III, iii, 1.
37. Ibid., III, iii, 1; IV, xxvi, 2.
38. Tertullian, *De praescriptione Haereticorum*, xx-xxi.